50 GREAT PUZZLES ON DEFENCE

The bidding is over, the opening lead has been made and, as soon as dummy appears, the time has come to assess your prospects in defence.

Ask yourself these questions every time until it has become second nature. How many high-card points are in dummy? How many do you have? Deduct the total from 40. How many points are missing? How many does declarer figure to have? You can often assess declarer's total points within a narrow range. If so, it follows that you can place partner's points also within a narrow range. You should also note whether dummy is minimum for the bidding or has extra strength. You check how many tricks you can see in defence and where the extra tricks needed might be found.

These are the sort of questions that will face you in this book. Most of the deals arose in actual play. Many come from national and international championships. You might be able to do better than the defenders did at the table.

Ron Klinger is a leading international bridge teacher and has represented Australia in many world championships from 1976 to 2016. He has written over sixty books, some of which have been translated into Bulgarian, Chinese, Danish, French, Hebrew and Icelandic. He has written a daily bridge column in *The Sydney Morning Herald* and *The Sun-Herald* from 2002 to 2018. His column now appears only on weekends. He provides constant material for the quizzes and problems on the www.ronklingerbridge.com website and also contributes regularly to a number of bridge magazines.

By RON KLINGER *in the Master Bridge Series*

BASIC BRIDGE: *The Guide to Good Acol Bidding and Play*
BETTER BRIDGE WITH A BETTER MEMORY • BRIDGE IS FUN
THE POWER OF SHAPE • WHEN TO BID, WHEN TO PASS
*GUIDE TO BETTER CARD PLAY • PLAYING TO WIN AT BRIDGE
GUIDE TO BETTER ACOL BRIDGE • TEACH YOUR CHILD BRIDGE
GUIDE TO BETTER DUPLICATE BRIDGE
BRIDGE CONVENTIONS, DEFENCES AND COUNTERMEASURES
100 WINNING BRIDGE TIPS • 50 MORE WINNING BRIDGE TIPS
100 WINNING DUPLICATE TIPS • ACOL BRIDGE MADE EASY
THE MODERN LOSING TRICK COUNT • IMPROVE YOUR BRIDGE MEMORY
IMPROVE YOUR DECLARER PLAY AT NO-TRUMPS
IMPROVE YOUR PLAY AT TRUMP CONTRACTS
IMPROVE YOUR OPENING LEADS
IMPROVE YOUR SLAM BIDDING • 5-CARD MAJOR STAYMAN
RON KLINGER ANSWERS YOUR BRIDGE QUERIES
BASIC ACOL BRIDGE FLIPPER • ACOL BRIDGE FLIPPER
MODERN LOSING TRICK COUNT FLIPPER
MEMORY-AIDS AND USEFUL RULES FLIPPER
BID BETTER, MUCH BETTER AFTER OPENING 1 NO-TRUMP
TO WIN AT BRIDGE • †RIGHT THROUGH THE PACK AGAIN
PLAYING DOUBLED CONTRACTS • DEFENDING DOUBLED CONTRACTS

*Winner of the 1991 Book of the Year Award of the American Bridge Teachers' Association
†Winner of the 2009 International Bridge Press Association Book of the Year Award

with Andrew Kambites
UNDERSTANDING SLAM BIDDING
CARD PLAY MADE EASY 3: *Trump Management*

with Hugh Kelsey
NEW INSTANT GUIDE TO BRIDGE

with Mike Lawrence
OPENING LEADS FOR ACOL PLAYERS

with Derek Rimington
IMPROVE YOUR BIDDING AND PLAY

with David Jackson
BETTER BALANCED BIDDING

with Roger Trézel and Terence Reese
THE MISTAKES YOU MAKE AT BRIDGE

with Wladyslaw Izdebski and Roman Krzemien
DEADLY DEFENCE • THE DEADLY DEFENCE QUIZ BOOK

with Wladyslaw Izdebski, Dariusz Kardas and Wlodzimierz Krysztofczyk
THE POWER OF POSITIVE BIDDING

50 GREAT PUZZLES ON DEFENCE

Ron Klinger

IN ASSOCIATION WITH
PETER CRAWLEY

First published in Great Britain 2019
in association with Peter Crawley
by Weidenfeld & Nicolson
an imprint of the Orion Publishing Group Ltd
Carmelite House, 50 Victoria Embankment, London EC4Y 0DZ

An Hachette UK Company

1 3 5 7 9 10 8 6 4 2

A CIP catalogue record for this book is available from the British Library.

ISBN: 978 1 474 61180 0

Typeset by Modern Bridge Publications
P.O. Box 140, Northbridge NSW 1560, Australia

Printed and bound in Great Britain by
Clays Ltd, Elcograf S.p.A

MIX
Paper from
responsible sources
FSC® C104740

www.orionbooks.co.uk

Contents

Introduction

Defending is much tougher than declarer play. For declarer, all the assets are revealed. For the defenders, only half of their assets are known to each player. They need to deduce from the values in dummy and the bidding where the defensive tricks to beat the contract can be found.

The opponents play varying methods, just as happens in real life. Any explanations that you need about the bidding are given.

If the setting is 'Teams', your objective is usually to beat the contract, but occasionally it might be to limit overtricks. When the setting is 'Pairs', the objective might be to restrict the overtricks, but naturally you want to defeat the contract if possible.

In each problem, you are given the auction and the opening lead, plus any early relevant play. Many of the problems deal with signalling. You might be required to give accurate signals to partner or to decipher partner's signals. On many occasions, suit-preference signals appear. You need to pay attention to the cards partner plays.

You should try to solve the problem yourself before going to the full deal and the solution on the next page. The answers include the reasoning that would enable you to find the right play.

Most of the deals arose in actual play and some occurred in national and international events. In many cases, the winning defence was not found.

A good idea in an actual tournament is to open this book about 45 minutes before play starts and tackle a few of the problems. Like an athlete warms up, so you can also warm up your 'little grey cells' and be ready to do your best on the very first board.

Ron Klinger, 2019

1. Teams: Dealer North : Nil vulnerable

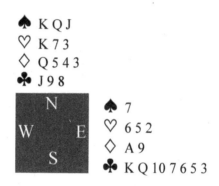

♠ K Q J
♡ K 7 3
♢ Q 5 4 3
♣ J 9 8

♠ 7
♡ 6 5 2
♢ A 9
♣ K Q 10 7 6 5 3

West	North	East	South
	1♢	3♣ (1)	3♡
3♠	4♡	All pass	

(1) Weak jump-overcall

West leads the ♣A. What should East play?

1. Teams: Dealer North : Nil vulnerable

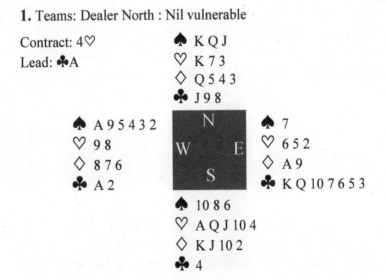

Contract: 4♡   ♠ K Q J
Lead: ♣A   ♡ K 7 3
                        ◇ Q 5 4 3
                        ♣ J 9 8

♠ A 9 5 4 3 2   ♠ 7
♡ 9 8   ♡ 6 5 2
◇ 8 7 6   ◇ A 9
♣ A 2   ♣ K Q 10 7 6 5 3

                 ♠ 10 8 6
                 ♡ A Q J 10 4
                 ◇ K J 10 2
                 ♣ 4

After the ♣A lead, there is little point encouraging clubs. If West has a second club, declarer will ruff. If you play high-encourage, play the ♣3 to ask for a switch. If you play low-encourage, play a high club, perhaps the ♣10, to ask for a switch.

Another option for East is a suit-preference signal, preferably with the ♣Q, an impossible natural card. If West reads that as asking for spades, ♠A and another spade will beat the contract. If West shifts to a diamond (the eight is best, to deny any interest in a diamond return), East wins and switches to spades to receive the killing ruff. With K-x-x or K-x-x-x in diamonds, leading the lowest diamond would suggest a diamond return.

In practice, West played a second club. South ruffed, drew trumps and knocked out the other two aces. As the cards lay there was no problem for declarer after trick 2.

Bridge journalese: 'Could do better' = 'Could hardly do worse'.

2. Teams: Dealer East : Both vulnerable

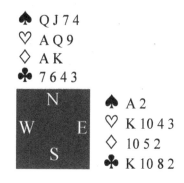

    ♠ Q J 7 4
    ♡ A Q 9
    ♢ A K
    ♣ 7 6 4 3

    ♠ A 2
    ♡ K 10 4 3
    ♢ 10 5 2
    ♣ K 10 8 2

West	North	East	South
		Pass	2♠ (1)
Pass	4♠	All pass	

(1) Weak two, six spades, 6-10 points

West leads the ♣Q. Which card should East play?

2. Teams: Dealer East : Both vulnerable

Contract: 4♠
Lead: ♣Q

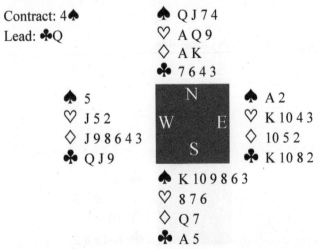

```
                    ♠ Q J 7 4
                    ♡ A Q 9
                    ◇ A K
                    ♣ 7 6 4 3

    ♠ 5             N              ♠ A 2
    ♡ J 5 2                        ♡ K 10 4 3
    ◇ J 9 8 6 4 3  W      E        ◇ 10 5 2
    ♣ Q J 9             S          ♣ K 10 8 2

                    ♠ K 10 9 8 6 3
                    ♡ 8 7 6
                    ◇ Q 7
                    ♣ A 5
```

Accurate signalling can be a delicate matter. There is a natural temptation for East to encourage clubs, but this is short-sighted. What East wants is a heart and so East should discourage clubs.

If West shifts to the ♡2 and declarer inserts the ♡9, East should play the ♡10. The ♡2, the lowest heart, indicates an honour in hearts, obviously the jack. The ♡10 wins and East will come to a second heart trick later. If declarer plays the ♡Q, East wins with the ♡K and returns the ♡3 to the jack and ace. East later collects the ♣K and the ♡10.

If East encourages clubs, South might duck trick 1 and a second club from West will be fatal. South wins and leads a trump. South can now easily draw trumps, eliminate diamonds and ruff dummy's clubs. A heart to the ♡9 will then endplay East.

Signal: A card played by a defender in the vain hope that partner is watching.

3. Pairs: Dealer East : Nil vulnerable

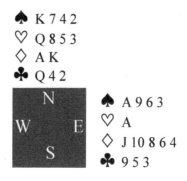

♠ K 7 4 2
♡ Q 8 5 3
♦ A K
♣ Q 4 2

♠ A 9 6 3
♡ A
♦ J 10 8 6 4
♣ 9 5 3

West	North	East	South
		Pass	2♡ (1)
3♣	3♡ (2)	4♣	4♡
Pass	Pass	Pass	

(1) Weak two, six hearts, 6-10 points
(2) Mild game invitation

West leads the ♣A: two – nine (reverse count) – ten and switches to the ♠8: two – ace – jack. What next?

3. Pairs: Dealer East : Nil vulnerable

Contract: 4♡
Lead: ♣A

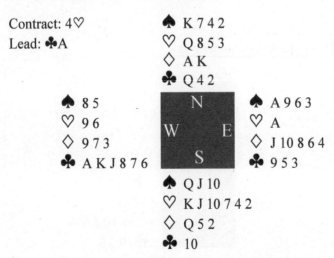

                  ♠ K 7 4 2
                  ♡ Q 8 5 3
                  ♢ A K
                  ♣ Q 4 2

♠ 8 5   ♠ A 9 6 3
♡ 9 6   ♡ A
♢ 9 7 3   ♢ J 10 8 6 4
♣ A K J 8 7 6   ♣ 9 5 3

                  ♠ Q J 10
                  ♡ K J 10 7 4 2
                  ♢ Q 5 2
                  ♣ 10

After the ♣A lead and ♠8 switch, won by the ♠A, East reverted
to clubs, hoping West had started with five clubs only. South
ruffed, knocked out the ♡A and had ten tricks. East-West made
their three aces, but no more.

At trick 3, East should return a spade. When West plays the ♠5,
East knows West began with a doubleton spade. Initially, the ♠8
could be a singleton (possible, but unlikely), top from a doubleton
or bottom from ♠Q-10-8. On coming in with the ♡A, East can
give West a spade ruff.

South's ♠J could not be a singleton. That would mean West had
led the ♠8 from ♠Q-10-8-5. Impossible. From that, West would
lead the ♠5 (normal choice) or possibly the ♠Q.

If West shows a spade doubleton, the rest is easy. If it transpires
that West began with ♠Q-10-8, the spade return does no harm.
East can still play for a second club trick when in with the ♡A.

*Finding the right switch: The sooner you leave an obnoxious
partner for a pleasant one.*

4. Teams: Dealer East : Nil vulnerable

♠ 10 5 3
♡ J 10
♢ K Q J 5 4 2
♣ A 7

♠ J 2
♡ Q 9
♢ A 9 6
♣ 9 8 6 5 4 2

West	North	East	South
		Pass	1♡
2♠ (1)	3♢	Pass	3♡
Pass	4♡	All pass	

(1) Weak jump-overcall

West leads the ♠A, ♠K, winning, and the ♠Q. What card should East play on that?

4. Teams: Dealer East : Nil vulnerable

Contract: 4♡
Lead: ♠A

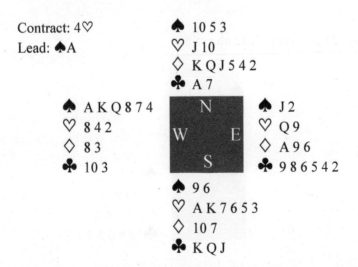

♠ 10 5 3
♡ J 10
◇ K Q J 5 4 2
♣ A 7

♠ A K Q 8 7 4
♡ 8 4 2
◇ 8 3
♣ 10 3

♠ J 2
♡ Q 9
◇ A 9 6
♣ 9 8 6 5 4 2

♠ 9 6
♡ A K 7 6 5 3
◇ 10 7
♣ K Q J

West has shown up with ♠A-K-Q, 9 HCP. East cannot expect anything more of substance from West, given the weak jump-overcall. East has one trick with the ◇A, but where will the defence find a fourth trick?

East should ruff West's ♠Q with the ♡9. That cannot hurt. The ♡Q was doomed anyway.

If East discards on the third spade, South ruffs, crosses to the ♣A and leads the ♡J: queen – ace – two. After a low heart to the ten, South returns to hand with a club, draws West's last trump and concedes a diamond.

When East ruffs the ♠Q with the ♡9, South over-ruffs with the ♡K. South crosses to the ♣A and plays the ♡J: queen – king – two and a heart to dummy's ♡10. West's ♡8 has become the top trump and the contract is one down.

Post mortem: Torture rivalled only by the Spanish Inquisition.

5. Teams: Dealer South : Nil vulnerable

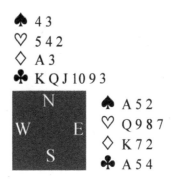

```
                    ♠ 4 3
                    ♡ 5 4 2
                    ◇ A 3
                    ♣ K Q J 10 9 3
                              ♠ A 5 2
                              ♡ Q 9 8 7
                              ◇ K 7 2
                              ♣ A 5 4
```

West	North	East	South
			1NT
Pass	3NT	All pass	

West leads the ♠J: three – ace – six. What do you play next?

5. Teams: Dealer South : Nil vulnerable

Contract: 3NT   ♠ 4 3
Lead: ♠J   ♡ 5 4 2
                    ♢ A 3
                    ♣ K Q J 10 9 3

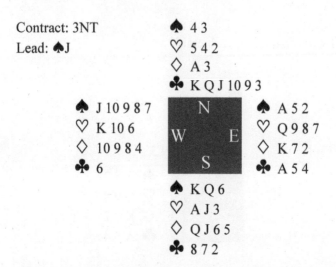

♠ J 10 9 8 7   ♠ A 5 2
♡ K 10 6   ♡ Q 9 8 7
♢ 10 9 8 4   ♢ K 7 2
♣ 6   ♣ A 5 4

                    ♠ K Q 6
                    ♡ A J 3
                    ♢ Q J 6 5
                    ♣ 8 7 2

West's ♠J lead could be from a suit headed by K-J-10, but it is much more likely that South began with the king-queen in spades. If you return a spade, South wins, knocks out the ♣A and has five clubs, two spades, a heart and a diamond.

A sensible plan is to try to nullify dummy's club suit. A low diamond at trick 2 will work if West has the ♢Q, but South is much more likely to have that card. Ask not what your partner can do for you when you can just do it yourself by playing the ♢K at trick 2. If declarer ducks this, continue with a low diamond. Now, as long as East ducks clubs twice, declarer has only eight tricks.

Switching to the ♢K does not come with guarantees. South could have ♢Q-J-10-x and playing the ♢K gives South the contract, but the ♢K play is a much better chance than returning a spade.

For every action, there is an equal and opposite criticism.

6. Teams: Dealer West : Nil vulnerable

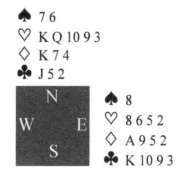

♠ 7 6
♡ K Q 10 9 3
♢ K 7 4
♣ J 5 2

♠ 8
♡ 8 6 5 2
♢ A 9 5 2
♣ K 10 9 3

West	North	East	South
1♢	1♡	2♢	2♠
3♢	Pass	Pass	3♠
Pass	Pass	Pass	

West leads the ♢Q: king – ace – six. What should East play next?

6. Teams: Dealer West : Nil vulnerable

Contract: 3♠
Lead: ◇Q

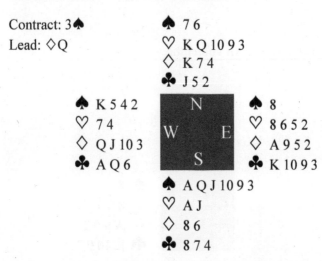

```
                    ♠ 7 6
                    ♡ K Q 10 9 3
                    ◇ K 7 4
                    ♣ J 5 2
     ♠ K 5 4 2              ♠ 8
     ♡ 7 4                  ♡ 8 6 5 2
     ◇ Q J 10 3             ◇ A 9 5 2
     ♣ A Q 6                ♣ K 10 9 3
                    ♠ A Q J 10 9 3
                    ♡ A J
                    ◇ 8 6
                    ♣ 8 7 4
```

After ◇Q – king – ace – six, East returned the ◇2. West won with the ◇10 and played the ◇J. South ruffed and deduced East must have the ♣K, as West did not lead a club initially. Hence, the ♠K must be with West. South played the ♠9, which won, and the ♠A. South cashed the ♡A, to give the impression that it was a singleton, and continued with ♠Q, pitching the ♡9 from dummy.

West won and, thinking South had no entry to dummy, played the ◇3. South ruffed, drew the last trump, overtook the ♡J in dummy and discarded two clubs on the heart winners, thus making 3♠.

Well done, South, but East had many opportunities to defeat 3♠. East could give count in hearts and play encouraging discards in clubs on the spades, but really, East should have solved the problem much earlier. At trick 1, East can see at best one heart trick and two diamonds for the defence. Where are the other tricks needed? East should definitely switch to the ♣3 at trick 2.

When I talk to partner about finding the right shift, he thinks I'm talking about clothing.

7. Teams: Dealer North : East-West vulnerable

```
              ♠ 10 8 3
              ♡ 4 3
              ◇ A Q J 9 5
              ♣ A Q 10
                             ♠ A J 6 2
                             ♡ A 8 7 6 2
                             ◇ 7 6 4
                             ♣ 7
```

West	North	East	South
	1◇	1♡	3NT
Pass	Pass	Pass	

West leads the ♡J. Plan East's defence.

Suppose East plays the HA and South follows with the HQ. What should East play next?

7. Teams: Dealer North : East-West vulnerable

Contract: 3NT
Lead: ♡J

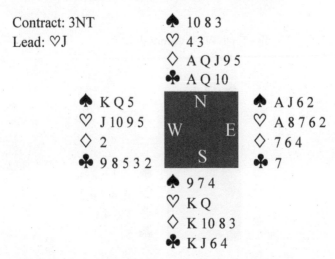

```
              ♠ 10 8 3
              ♡ 4 3
              ◇ A Q J 9 5
              ♣ A Q 10
♠ K Q 5                      ♠ A J 6 2
♡ J 10 9 5         N         ♡ A 8 7 6 2
◇ 2            W       E      ◇ 7 6 4
♣ 9 8 5 3 2        S         ♣ 7
              ♠ 9 7 4
              ♡ K Q
              ◇ K 10 8 3
              ♣ K J 6 4
```

Defending becomes easier if you focus on the tricks you need. Just as declarer has a contract, consider that you also have a contract when you are defending. South is in 3NT. Your contract, to defeat 3NT, is five tricks. Where can they come from?

One look at dummy tells you that you are not collecting any tricks from clubs. At trick 1, you can place South with ♡K-Q. South needs only the ♣K and ◇10-x or ◇K and ♣J-x to make nine tricks. South might have ♡K-Q bare, but might also have played the ♡Q from ♡K-Q-10 or ♡K-Q-9 to tempt you to return a heart.

If South has a spade winner, you will not beat 3NT. You need to hope partner has values in spades. Switch to the ♠2 at trick 2. A low-card switch asks partner to return the suit you are leading. You can now collect four spade tricks for one down. It is bad enough that you have missed the cold 4♡ on your meagre, combined values. You must not increase the damage by letting South make 3NT.

Real men bid without values.

8. Teams: Dealer South : East-West vulnerable

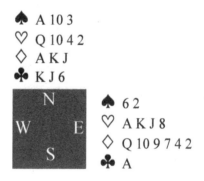

♠ A 10 3
♡ Q 10 4 2
◇ A K J
♣ K J 6

♠ 6 2
♡ A K J 8
◇ Q 10 9 7 4 2
♣ A

West	North	East	South
			Pass
Pass	1♣	1◇	1♡
Pass	2NT (1)	Pass	3♠ (2)
Pass	4♡	Double	All pass

(1) 18-20 points, balanced shape
(2) 4-4 in the majors

West leads the ◇6, taken by the ace. Declarer plays the ♣K from dummy. What would you play as East at trick 3?

8. Teams: Dealer South : East-West vulnerable

Contract: 4♡ doubled
Lead: ◇6

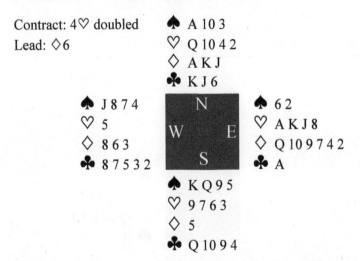

♠ A 10 3
♡ Q 10 4 2
◇ A K J
♣ K J 6

♠ J 8 7 4
♡ 5
◇ 8 6 3
♣ 8 7 5 3 2

♠ 6 2
♡ A K J 8
◇ Q 10 9 7 4 2
♣ A

♠ K Q 9 5
♡ 9 7 6 3
◇ 5
♣ Q 10 9 4

South is known to be 4-4 in the majors. Playing the ♣K means South has the ♣Q. In that case, the ♣A is your only trick there. With no high cards in the red suits, South should have ♠K-J-x-x or ♠K-Q-x-x. In either case, a spade switch at trick 3 is futile.

You have 4♡ doubled one down, but more is better. A useful principle with trump length when the opponents are in a 4-4 or 5-3 fit is to force declarer to ruff. 'Trump length, lead length'. East should play a high diamond at trick 3 (not an instinctive move).

Dummy wins and plays a low heart. The ♡J wins and East returns a diamond, won in dummy. East takes the next heart, followed by a fourth diamond, ruffed. Whether ruffed in dummy or in hand, South is left with one heart opposite two. Another heart would be won by East and the fifth diamond takes 4♡ three down for +500 E-W. South should abandon trumps and lead winners. East ruffs a black suit with ♡8 for two down and +300. If East plays anything but a diamond at trick 3, declarer can escape for one down.

Every bridge mishap is funny as long as it is happening to somebody else.

9. Teams: Dealer North : East-West vulnerable

♠ 3
♡ A J 10 6
◇ Q 8 5
♣ A K J 10 7

♠ A 9 7 5
♡ 8 7 3
◇ K 4
♣ 8 6 4 3

West	North	East	South
	1♣	Pass	1♡
Pass	3♡	Pass	4♡
Pass	Pass	Pass	

West leads the ♠4: three – ace – jack. What next?

9. Teams: Dealer North : East-West vulnerable

Contract: 4♡
Lead: ♠4

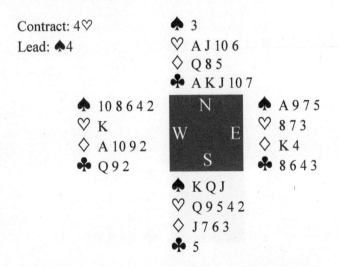

♠ 3
♡ A J 10 6
◇ Q 8 5
♣ A K J 10 7

♠ 10 8 6 4 2   ♠ A 9 7 5
♡ K   ♡ 8 7 3
◇ A 10 9 2   ◇ K 4
♣ Q 9 2   ♣ 8 6 4 3

♠ K Q J
♡ Q 9 5 4 2
◇ J 7 6 3
♣ 5

This is easy if you just ask yourself the question every defender should ask as soon as dummy appears: Where are our tricks?

You have one spade trick. There are no more tricks from the spades, none from the clubs and almost certainly none from the hearts. If South has the ◇A, there is no hope. Any diamond losers could then be pitched via dummy's club suit.

It is usually unattractive to lead from a king-high suit when dummy has the queen, but needs must. East should switch boldly to the ◇K at trick 2. West wins the next diamond and the third diamond is ruffed by East for one down.

If you switched to the ◇K at trick 2 almost instantaneously, then your defensive thinking is on the right track.

Fame is the proof that people are gullible.
(Ralph Waldo Emerson)

10. Teams: Dealer North : North-South vulnerable

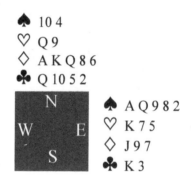

```
              ♠ 10 4
              ♡ Q 9
              ◇ A K Q 8 6
              ♣ Q 10 5 2
         N                ♠ A Q 9 8 2
     W       E            ♡ K 7 5
         S                ◇ J 9 7
                          ♣ K 3
```

West	North	East	South
	1◇	1♠	2♡
2♠ (1)	3♣ (2)	Pass	3♡
Pass	4♡	All pass	

(1) 3-card raise
(2) Double for takeout is a better choice.

West leads the ♠5. Plan the defence for East.

10. Teams: Dealer East : Both vulnerable

Contract: 4 ♡   ♠ 10 4
Lead: ♠5   ♡ Q 9
                                ◇ A K Q 8 6
                                ♣ Q 10 5 2

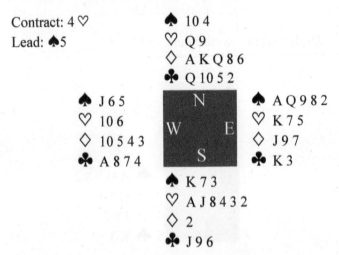

♠ J 6 5		♠ A Q 9 8 2
♡ 10 6		♡ K 7 5
◇ 10 5 4 3		◇ J 9 7
♣ A 8 7 4		♣ K 3

                                ♠ K 7 3
                                ♡ A J 8 4 3 2
                                ◇ 2
                                ♣ J 9 6

Win trick 1 with the ♠A and shift to ♣K at trick 2. Continue with
the ♣3 to the ace and receive a club ruff to take 4♡ one down.

How can East tell? If South has ♠K and ♣A, there is no hope.
For the 2♡ bid, South should have at least one of the ♣A and
♠K. If South has ♣A and West ♠K, East can play ♠Q and a
third spade, forcing dummy to ruff and ensuring a trump trick, but
that is only one heart and two spade tricks. If South has the ♣A,
the defence is hamstrung. East needs to play West for the ♣A and
either receive a club ruff or a trump trick if West has the ♣A and
♡J-x.

This arose in a National Butler Trials (pairs scored by Imps).
Open datum: N-S 90. Women's datum: N-S 70. If you switched to
the ♣K, you collect 5 Imps. On any other return, you lose 11
Imps. Seniors datum: N-S 280. You win 9 Imps for the ♣K switch
and lose 8 Imps for any other play.

*An Englishman thinks seated, a Frenchman, standing, an
American, pacing, and a bridge player afterwards.*

11. Teams: Dealer South : North-South vulnerable

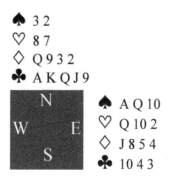

♠ 3 2
♡ 8 7
◇ Q 9 3 2
♣ A K Q J 9

♠ A Q 10
♡ Q 10 2
◇ J 8 5 4
♣ 10 4 3

West	North	East	South
			1♡
Pass	2♣	Pass	2♡
Pass	3◇	Pass	3♡
Pass	4♡	All pass	

West leads the ♠5, fourth-highest if from a 4-card or longer suit.
Plan the defence for East.

11. Teams: Dealer South : North-South vulnerable

Contract: 4♡
Lead: ♠5

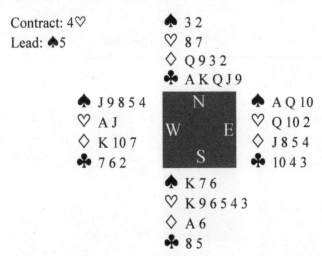

East knows there are no club tricks for the defence and at best one diamond. West would have led a top diamond from ◇A-K. East can see that there are two spade tricks at best and one diamond trick. If West has the ♠K, then East can hope that West also has the ◇K or ◇A and the ♡J. If West does not have the ♠K, East knows that the defence will need two tricks from the hearts.

Play the ♠Q at trick 1. If it wins, cash ♠A and switch to a diamond. You hope for a diamond trick and a heart trick or two heart tricks. When South wins trick 1 and returns a spade, East wins. Needing two heart tricks, East switches to a low heart. The defence can take two heart tricks and cash another spade.

Note that it does not help declarer to win the ♠K and start running the clubs. West can ruff the fourth club, cash the ♡A and exit with a spade. The defence will come to three heart tricks and a diamond trick later.

What do bridge players do after a tough day's bridge?
They wine down.

12. Teams: Dealer West : Both vulnerable

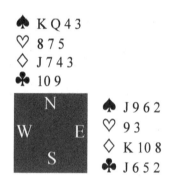

♠ K Q 4 3
♡ 8 7 5
◇ J 7 4 3
♣ 10 9

♠ J 9 6 2
♡ 9 3
◇ K 10 8
♣ J 6 5 2

West	North	East	South
1◇	Pass	1♠	4♡
Pass	Pass	Pass	

West leads the ♠A. What card should East play on that?
West switches to the ◇2: three – king – five.
What should East play next?

12. Teams: Dealer West : Both vulnerable

Contract: 4♡
Lead: ♠A

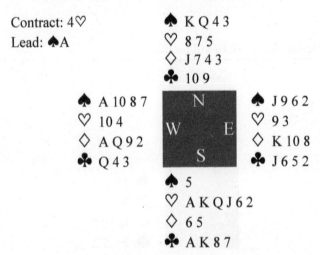

	♠ K Q 4 3
	♡ 8 7 5
	◇ J 7 4 3
	♣ 10 9

♠ A 10 8 7   ♠ J 9 6 2
♡ 10 4   ♡ 9 3
◇ A Q 9 2   ◇ K 10 8
♣ Q 4 3   ♣ J 6 5 2

♠ 5
♡ A K Q J 6 2
◇ 6 5
♣ A K 8 7

Even though East had bid spades, the ♣A lead holds little appeal. A low club is at least as good and might be better.

As a spade continuation is undesirable, which both defenders know, East should play the ♠9 or the ♠J, not as encouraging or discouraging, but as suit-preference for diamonds.

In a World Open Teams, one West switched to the ◇A and a second diamond to the king. South made the rest for +420. At the other table, West switched to ◇2, hoping to find East with ◇K-x (for a diamond ruff). The ◇K won, but East shifted to a club. South made 11 tricks via ♣A, ♡A, ♡K, ♣K, club ruff, ♠K, ♠Q, +450, +1 Imp, which was the winning margin in the match.

There are two clues for East to return a diamond. (1) A low card switch (◇2) asks partner to return that suit. (2) When the ◇K won, East can place West with the ◇A. Had West wanted a club switch, West would play ◇A and then a low diamond to East.

Play by third hand on the first trick: The second chance for the defence to blunder.

13. Pairs: Dealer East : Nil vulnerable

♠ A J 9 7 5 4 3 2
♡ 5
◇ 10 8 5 2
♣ ---

♠ Q 8 6
♡ A K 2
◇ K J
♣ 9 8 7 4 2

West	North	East	South
		1♣	1NT (1)
2♡ (2)	3♡ (3)	Double	3♠
4♡	4♠	5♡	Double
Pass	5♠	All pass	

(1) 15-18, balanced
(2) Natural, not forcing
(3) Transfer to spades

West leads the ♡J: five – king – three. What next?

13. Pairs: Dealer East : Nil vulnerable

Contract: 5♠
Lead: ♡J

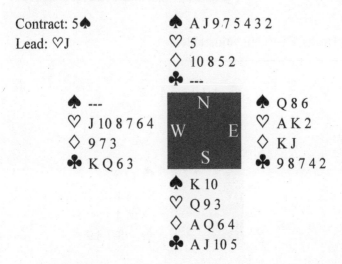

♠ A J 9 7 5 4 3 2
♡ 5
♢ 10 8 5 2
♣ ---

♠ ---
♡ J 10 8 7 6 4
♢ 9 7 3
♣ K Q 6 3

♠ Q 8 6
♡ A K 2
♢ K J
♣ 9 8 7 4 2

♠ K 10
♡ Q 9 3
♢ A Q 6 4
♣ A J 10 5

If East returns a heart or switches to a club, declarer wins and plays ♠K, ♠A. Then a low diamond from dummy picks up the whole diamond suit and South makes eleven tricks.

Switching to the ♢K will work if West had the ♢A, but there is a better move, which may work in other situations as well.

The great Tim Seres of Australia (1925-2007) switched to the ♢J at trick 2! What was South to do? Playing the ♢Q would look silly if West won and gave East a diamond ruff. Rising with the ♢A would be successful if trumps were 2-1 or if West had all three. South did rise with the ♢A and played the ♠K. One down.

It is true that if West had the ♢A, switching to the ♢K produces two down if East can ruff the third diamond without being over-ruffed, but your #1 aim at teams is to defeat the contract.

What's the difference between teams and pairs strategy?
Answer: At teams you have to justify your actions to three players instead of just one.

14. Teams: Dealer East : Both vulnerable

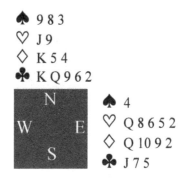

♠ 9 8 3
♡ J 9
♢ K 5 4
♣ K Q 9 6 2

♠ 4
♡ Q 8 6 5 2
♢ Q 10 9 2
♣ J 7 5

West	North	East	South
		Pass	1♠
2♡	2♠	4♡	4♠
Pass	Pass	Pass	

West leads the ♡A: nine from dummy . . . What would you play as East?

14. Teams: Dealer East : Both vulnerable

Contract: 4♠   ♠ 9 8 3
Lead: ♡A   ♡ J 9
                               ◇ K 5 4
                               ♣ K Q 9 6 2

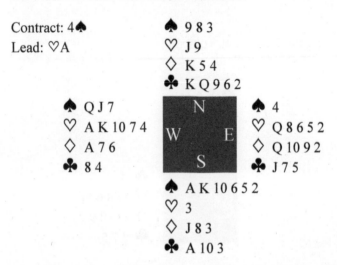

♠ Q J 7   ♠ 4
♡ A K 10 7 4   ♡ Q 8 6 5 2
◇ A 7 6   ◇ Q 10 9 2
♣ 8 4   ♣ J 7 5

                               ♠ A K 10 6 5 2
                               ♡ 3
                               ◇ J 8 3
                               ♣ A 10 3

East knows that a heart continuation is futile, as declarer will ruff the next heart (if not this one). East should discourage hearts, but it needs to be a dramatic card to ask for a diamond switch. The best chance to excite partner's attention is to play the ♡Q at trick 1. Partner should read this as asking for a diamond (high card for the higher outside suit, excluding trumps).

As long as West shifts to a diamond at trick 2, the defence can score four tricks (one spade, a heart and two diamonds). If West plays a heart at trick 2 (or a club or a spade), declarer can make ten tricks.

On the existing layout, it does not matter here whether West plays ◇A and a second diamond or switches to a low diamond. The low diamond can work better if East began with ◇Q-x and declarer plays low from dummy. East wins and returns the other diamond. West wins and if East can ruff the third diamond, 4♠ is two down.

Ancora imparo ('I am still learning')
A favourite saying of Michelangelo.

15. Teams: Dealer North : North-South vulnerable

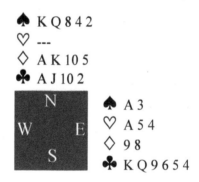

♠ K Q 8 4 2
♡ ---
♢ A K 10 5
♣ A J 10 2

♠ A 3
♡ A 5 4
♢ 9 8
♣ K Q 9 6 5 4

West	North	East	South
	1♠	2♣	2♡
Pass	3♢	Pass	3♡
Pass	3NT	Pass	4♡
Pass	Pass	Pass	

West leads the ♠J: king – ace – five. What would you do as East?

15. Teams: Dealer North : North-South vulnerable

Contract: 4♡
Lead: ♠J

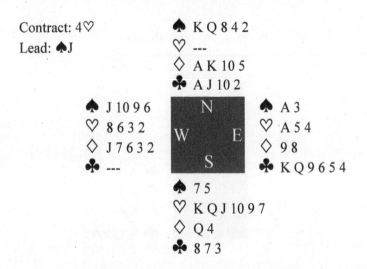

♠ K Q 8 4 2
♡ ---
◇ A K 10 5
♣ A J 10 2

♠ J 10 9 6
♡ 8 6 3 2
◇ J 7 6 3 2
♣ ---

♠ A 3
♡ A 5 4
◇ 9 8
♣ K Q 9 6 5 4

♠ 7 5
♡ K Q J 10 9 7
◇ Q 4
♣ 8 7 3

South removed 3NT to 4♡, as the hearts might be (and would be) useless in no-trumps. East switched to the ♣K at trick 2 (any club would do, as it happens). West ruffed and played another spade, taken by the ♠Q. After ◇5 to the ◇Q, South played a top heart, East won and reverted to clubs. West ruffed and 4♡ was one off.

To defeat 4♡, the defence needs to collect two club ruffs. A mechanical spade at trick 2 ('return partner's lead'), allows South to succeed. South takes the ♠Q, comes to hand with the ◇Q and plays a top heart. The defence can now take only one spade, one heart and one club ruff.

How did East know to play a club at trick 2? By asking a simple question, 'Why would partner lead a spade, a suit bid by dummy, and not a club, the suit that I bid?' Answer: Partner is probably void in clubs. Did the opening lead leap out at you, too?

Competitive decision: Justified if made by you, an overbid if made by partner.

16. Pairs: Dealer South : North-South vulnerable

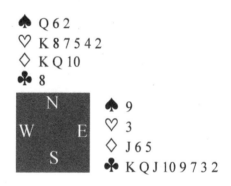

♠ Q 6 2
♡ K 8 7 5 4 2
♢ K Q 10
♣ 8

♠ 9
♡ 3
♢ J 6 5
♣ K Q J 10 9 7 3 2

West	North	East	South
			1♡
1♠	2NT (1)	5♣	Pass
Pass	5♡	All pass	

(1) 4+ hearts, forcing to game

West leads the ♣A. What card would you play on that as East?

16. Pairs: Dealer South : North-South vulnerable

Contract: 5♡
Lead: ♣A

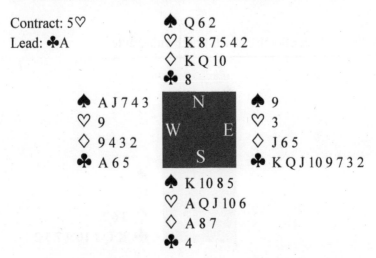

♠ Q 6 2
♡ K 8 7 5 4 2
♢ K Q 10
♣ 8

♠ A J 7 4 3
♡ 9
♢ 9 4 3 2
♣ A 6 5

♠ 9
♡ 3
♢ J 6 5
♣ K Q J 10 9 7 3 2

♠ K 10 8 5
♡ A Q J 10 6
♢ A 8 7
♣ 4

Bidding on to 5♡ was dangerous. Doubling 5♣ could give North-South +300 via one heart trick and three diamond tricks.

The ♠A lead, followed by a second spade, would put paid to 5♡. East ruffs and a club switch gives East-West three tricks. After the ♣A, switching to ♠A and another spade also works. This is not far-fetched. East is hardly likely to have three spades and might easily have a singleton.

East should help West find the spade switch by playing the ♣K under the ♣A as a suit-preference signal (high card for the high suit). This works perfectly when West has the ♠A. If West has something like ♠K-J-x-x-x ♡x ♢A-x-x-x ♣A-x-x, West should not heed East's signal, but simply play ♢A and a second diamond and wait for the spade trick to come later.

It is unwise to reproach yourself regularly if this is likely to fan the flames of partner's baser instincts.

17. Teams: Dealer East : Both vulnerable

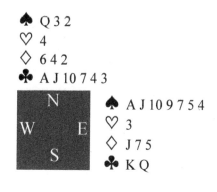

```
            ♠ Q 3 2
            ♡ 4
            ◇ 6 4 2
            ♣ A J 10 7 4 3
                            ♠ A J 10 9 7 5 4
                            ♡ 3
                            ◇ J 7 5
                            ♣ K Q
```

West	North	East	South
		1♠	4♡
Double (1)	Pass	Pass	Pass
(1) Penalties			

West leads the ♠K. What card would you play on that as East?

17. Teams: Dealer East : Both vulnerable

Contract: 4 ♡
Lead: ♠K

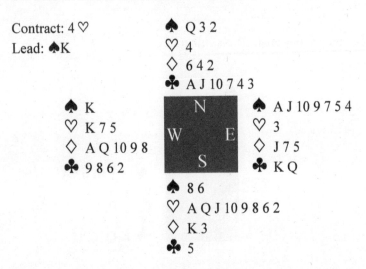

```
                    ♠ Q 3 2
                    ♡ 4
                    ◇ 6 4 2
                    ♣ A J 10 7 4 3
    ♠ K                           ♠ A J 10 9 7 5 4
    ♡ K 7 5          N            ♡ 3
    ◇ A Q 10 9 8   W   E          ◇ J 7 5
    ♣ 9 8 6 2        S            ♣ K Q
                    ♠ 8 6
                    ♡ A Q J 10 9 8 6 2
                    ◇ K 3
                    ♣ 5
```

There is no value in encouraging spades. If West has another spade, South will ruff it. Overtaking the ♠K and returning a spade works, but that is risky. East should play the ♠4. If West has a second spade and plays it, fine. If not, West should read the ♠4 as suit-preference for clubs. If West switches to a club, East-West can come to two spades, a heart and two diamonds.

In practice, East played the ♠7 at trick 1 and South the ♠8. West took the ♠7 as asking for diamonds, maybe from ♠A-7-6-5-4, and switched to ◇10. South won with the ◇K, cashed ♡A (♡7 from West) and played the ♡6 (♡5 from West). West won the third heart and cashed the ◇A. A club switch still beats 4♡, but West continued with ◇Q. South ruffed and ran trumps. With one trump to go, South had ♠6, ♡8, ♣5, dummy had ♠Q, ♣A-J and East had ♠A, ♣K-Q. When South played the ♡6, discarding the ♠Q from dummy, East was finished.

Bridge players do it with a squeeze.

18. Teams: Dealer South : North-South vulnerable

♠ ---
♡ Q 5
♢ 10 9 6 5 3
♣ A K Q 9 7 5

♠ K Q 8 7 4 3
♡ 9 7 3 2
♢ ---
♣ J 8 3

West	North	East	South
			1♡
2♢	3♣	Pass	3♡
Pass	4♡	All pass	

West leads the ♢K. What card would you play on that as East?

18. Teams: Dealer South : North-South vulnerable

Contract: 4♡
Lead: ◇K

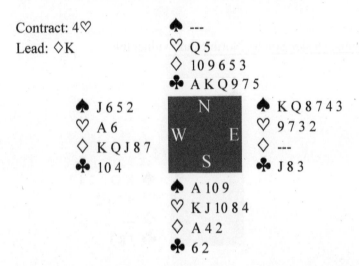

           ♠ ---
           ♡ Q 5
           ◇ 10 9 6 5 3
           ♣ A K Q 9 7 5

♠ J 6 5 2   ♠ K Q 8 7 4 3
♡ A 6   ♡ 9 7 3 2
◇ K Q J 8 7   ◇ ---
♣ 10 4   ♣ J 8 3

           ♠ A 10 9
           ♡ K J 10 8 4
           ◇ A 4 2
           ♣ 6 2

In the final of a National Seniors' Team Selection, East discarded the ♠3 (odd-encouraging) on West's ◇K lead. South won and played the ♡4 to the ♡Q. The ♡5 then went to South's ♡K and the ♡A. West cashed two diamonds and switched to ♠2. South won, drew trumps and had the rest, for +620, as dummy was high.

West can beat 4♡ by switching to a club when in with the ♡A or after cashing the ◇Q, but he thought East's ♠3 discard indicated the ace. East can beat 4♡ by pitching a club at trick 1. After the same line, ♡4 to ♡Q, ♡5 to ♡A, West cashes ◇Q, ◇J, on which East throws two more clubs. West now gives East a club ruff. Declarer has no winning line without help from the opponents.

At the other table, South opened 1♡, West doubled and, after a competitive auction, North reached 5♣ (unbeatable) and East sacrificed in 5♠, doubled by North. In the play, declarer took a ruffing finesse in diamonds and lost two clubs and one trick in each of the other suits. That was −500, but a gain of 3 Imps.

Different systems exist for discarding. Some bridge players play revolving discards, others play revolting discards.

19. Teams: Dealer East : East-West vulnerable

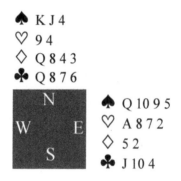

♠ K J 4
♡ 9 4
◇ Q 8 4 3
♣ Q 8 7 6

♠ Q 10 9 5
♡ A 8 7 2
◇ 5 2
♣ J 10 4

West	North	East	South
		Pass	1NT (1)
Pass	Pass	Pass	

(1) 12-14 points, balanced

1. West leads the ♡K: four – two (low-like) – five.
2. West continues with the ♡J: nine – eight – six.
3. West plays the ♡10: ◇3 – ♡A – ♣2.
4. East cashes the ♡7: ♠2 – ♡3 – ◇4.

What do you play as East at trick 5?

19. Teams: Dealer East : East-West vulnerable

Contract: 1NT
Lead: ♡K

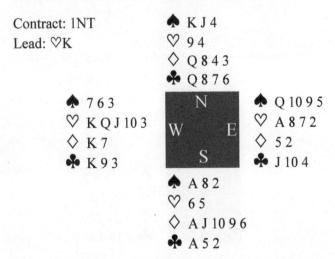

```
                    ♠ K J 4
                    ♡ 9 4
                    ◇ Q 8 4 3
                    ♣ Q 8 7 6
    ♠ 7 6 3            N              ♠ Q 10 9 5
    ♡ K Q J 10 3                      ♡ A 8 7 2
    ◇ K 7         W         E         ◇ 5 2
    ♣ K 9 3            S              ♣ J 10 4
                    ♠ A 8 2
                    ♡ 6 5
                    ◇ A J 10 9 6
                    ♣ A 5 2
```

Neither East-West found seven tricks against 1NT on this deal from the final of a National Open Teams. At both tables West led the ♡K, which won. What next?

Given time, declarer can make seven tricks via four diamonds, two spades and the ♣A. The defenders have five heart tricks and need to score the ♣K before West's ◇K has been forced out.

To show club interest, one West continued with ♡J and ♡10 to East's ♡A. When East returned ♡7, West followed with the ♡3. East shifted to a diamond, groan, and declarer made seven tricks. To ask for diamonds, West would play the highest honour each time: ♡K, then ♡Q, then ♡J. Lower honours = lower suit, clubs.

At the other table West played ♡10 at trick 2. East won with the ♡A and returned ♡7. West should follow with ♡3 and wait for East to switch to a club. No, West overtook ♡7 with the ♡J and could not defeat 1NT after cashing two more hearts. No swing.

Bridge vows: 'Will you promise to love, honour and obey partner's signals?' Required answer: 'I will.'

20. Teams: Dealer South : East-West vulnerable

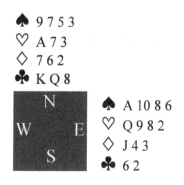

♠ 9 7 5 3
♡ A 7 3
◇ 7 6 2
♣ K Q 8

♠ A 10 8 6
♡ Q 9 8 2
◇ J 4 3
♣ 6 2

West	North	East	South
			1♠
Pass	2♠	Pass	3♣ (1)
Pass	4♠	All pass	

(1) Long-suit trial bid, 3+ clubs, seeking help in clubs

1. West leads the ♡J: ace – two (encouraging) – four.
2. The ♠3 comes from dummy: six – king – ♡5.
3. South plays the ♣3: four (reverse count) – king – two.
4. ♠5 from dummy: eight – jack – ♡6.
5. Declarer continues with the ♣7: five – queen – six.
6. South plays the ♣8 from dummy . . .

What would you play as East on the ♣8 at trick 6?

20. Teams: Dealer South : East-West vulnerable

Contract: 4♠
Lead: ♡J

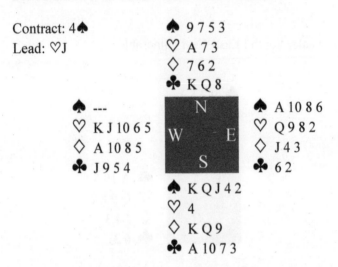

♠ 9 7 5 3
♡ A 7 3
◇ 7 6 2
♣ K Q 8

♠ ---
♡ K J 10 6 5
◇ A 10 8 5
♣ J 9 5 4

♠ A 10 8 6
♡ Q 9 8 2
◇ J 4 3
♣ 6 2

♠ K Q J 4 2
♡ 4
◇ K Q 9
♣ A 10 7 3

In the final of a National Open Teams, both Souths were in 4♠. The play began the same way: ♡J lead, taken by the ace; ♠3 to the king; ♣3 to the king; ♠5 to the jack; ♣7 to the queen, followed by the ♣8 from dummy.

East should simply discard on this club, but both defenders ruffed in prematurely. Now declarer was able to discard a diamond from dummy on the ♣A and lost only one diamond trick as well as two spades. No swing.

In situations such as this one, it could be right for East to ruff the loser if East needed the lead urgently to cash tricks or if declarer would be able to make a vital discard from dummy on the next round of the suit. Otherwise it is foolish for East to ruff the loser.

No swing on a board that was touch-and-go at both tables. It touched and went. (Edgar Kaplan)

21. Teams: Dealer South : Nil vulnerable

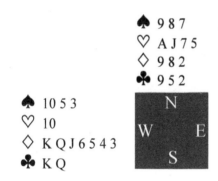

```
              ♠ 9 8 7
              ♡ A J 7 5
              ◇ 9 8 2
              ♣ 9 5 2
♠ 10 5 3          N
♡ 10         W         E
◇ K Q J 6 5 4 3
♣ K Q            S
```

West	North	East	South
			1♡
3◇ (1)	Pass	Pass	Double (2)
Pass	4♡	All pass	

(1) Weak jump-overcall, 6+ diamonds, 6-10 points
(2) Takeout double

West leads the ◇K: two – ten – seven. What next?

21. Teams: Dealer South : Nil vulnerable

Contract: 4♡
Lead: ◇K

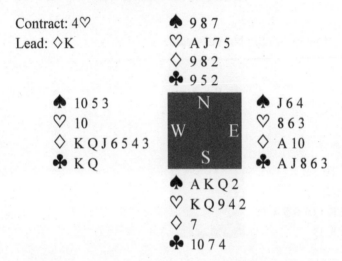

```
                    ♠ 9 8 7
                    ♡ A J 7 5
                    ◇ 9 8 2
                    ♣ 9 5 2
♠ 10 5 3                          ♠ J 6 4
♡ 10                             ♡ 8 6 3
◇ K Q J 6 5 4 3                  ◇ A 10
♣ K Q                            ♣ A J 8 6 3
                    ♠ A K Q 2
                    ♡ K Q 9 4 2
                    ◇ 7
                    ♣ 10 7 4
```

West knows that a second diamond is futile. South will simply ruff. With one trick in, the defence needs three more tricks. It is highly unlikely that East has ♠A-K, the only way to collect two tricks from the spades. Smaller prayers are easier to have answered. You do not need partner to have ♠A-K. ♣A-J will do.

West should switch to the ♣K at trick 2. East plays an encouraging signal and West continues with the ♣Q. East overtakes and cashes the ♣J to take 4♡ one down.

The defence also works if East has ♣A-x-x-x-x. Realizing that there can be only two club tricks for the defence if West began with ♣K-Q-x, East overtakes the ♣Q and returns a club, hoping West can ruff. If South ruffs the third club, the defence has not lost a trick.

Note that 4♡ makes if West continues diamonds at trick 2 or if East fails to overtake the ♣Q to cash the ♣J. South can then draw trumps and pitch a club loser from dummy on the thirteenth spade.

Be an overtaker, lest they call the undertaker.

22. Teams: Dealer South : Both vulnerable

♠ Q 8 6
♡ Q 8 7 5 3
♢ A Q J 8
♣ 10

♠ K J 4
♡ 4
♢ 10 9 4
♣ A Q 9 8 5 3

West	North	East	South
			1♡
2♣	4♣ (1)	5♣	5♡
Pass	Pass	Pass	

(1) Strong, 0-1 club, 4+ hearts

West leads the ♣A: ten – king – jack.

What should West play next?

22. Teams: Dealer South : Both vulnerable

Contract: 5♡
Lead: ♣A

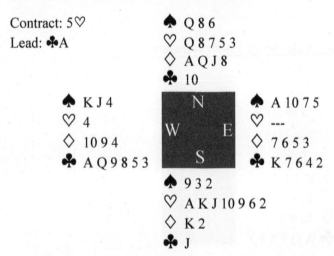

```
                        ♠ Q 8 6
                        ♡ Q 8 7 5 3
                        ◇ A Q J 8
                        ♣ 10
   ♠ K J 4                   N              ♠ A 10 7 5
   ♡ 4                                      ♡ ---
   ◇ 10 9 4           W         E           ◇ 7 6 5 3
   ♣ A Q 9 8 5 3              S             ♣ K 7 6 4 2
                        ♠ 9 3 2
                        ♡ A K J 10 9 6 2
                        ◇ K 2
                        ♣ J
```

In two tables in the semi-finals of a National Teams, West led the
♣A against 5♡. One East played a much too subtle ♣7. West
switched to the ◇10 and South made 11 tricks, +650.

At the other table, East played the ♣K at trick 1. This could
hardly cost. Even if South had the ♣Q, one discard from dummy
would not help South. The ♣K screams for a spade switch. It is
hard to find a clearer suit-preference signal, but West here also
switched to the 'safe' ◇10, no swing.

If West reads East's ♣K correctly, West should switch to ♠K and
continue with ♠J. This takes 5♡ two down. After the ♠K, West
should play ♠J next, not the ♠4. If West continues with the ♠4,
low from dummy, East will play the ♠A, not the ♠10. If you
switch to the ♠4 at trick 2 and dummy plays low, East will
probably play ♠A and return a spade. That takes 5♡ down, but
only by one trick.

Suit-preference signal: Your clever play, which is understood by
three players at the table. None of these is your partner.

23. Pairs: Dealer West : Nil vulnerable

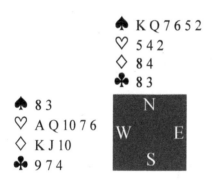

♠ K Q 7 6 5 2
♡ 5 4 2
◇ 8 4
♣ 8 3

♠ 8 3
♡ A Q 10 7 6
◇ K J 10
♣ 9 7 4

West	North	East	South
Pass	Pass	Pass	1♠
2♡	4♠	5♡	5♠
Pass	Pass	Pass	

West leads the ♡A: two – eight – king.

What would you play next?

23. Teams: Dealer West : East-West vulnerable

Contract: 5♠
Lead: ♡A

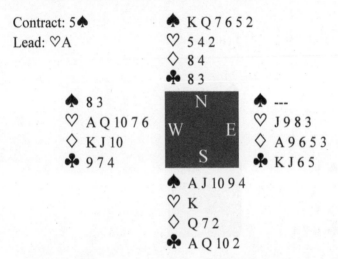

```
                    ♠ K Q 7 6 5 2
                    ♡ 5 4 2
                    ◇ 8 4
                    ♣ 8 3
    ♠ 8 3                              ♠ ---
    ♡ A Q 10 7 6         N            ♡ J 9 8 3
    ◇ K J 10        W         E       ◇ A 9 6 5 3
    ♣ 9 7 4              S            ♣ K J 6 5
                    ♠ A J 10 9 4
                    ♡ K
                    ◇ Q 7 2
                    ♣ A Q 10 2
```

West did well to lead ♡A. On a spade lead, South can make 5♠ by finessing the ♣10 and later the ♣Q. Similarly, 5♠ makes if West leads a club. South also did well to save in 5♠. It is unusual to bid five-over-five when the opponents who have bid to 5♡ are both passed hands, but 5♡ can succeed after any lead but a club.

As East knows South began with a singleton heart, attitude or count signals are pointless. A suit-preference signal is required. After trick 1, West knows East began with ♡J-9-8-3. The ♡J = diamond switch; ♡3 = club switch. What did East's ♡8 mean at trick 1?

West might take the ♡9 as high, requesting a diamond, but the ♡8 should mean useful holdings in both minors. East cannot tell which minor is best for West's switch. The ♡8 suggests a strong holding in both. West should switch to the suit where honours are held, here a diamond. On any shift but a diamond, 5♠ can make.

Rule of Restricted Talent: If you need to continue a suit to beat 3NT, you switch. If a switch is needed, you will continue the suit.

24. Pairs: Dealer West : East-West vulnerable

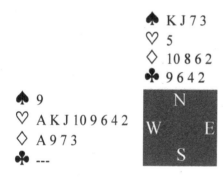

```
                    ♠ K J 7 3
                    ♡ 5
                    ♢ 10 8 6 2
                    ♣ 9 6 4 2
♠ 9
♡ A K J 10 9 6 4 2        N
♢ A 9 7 3          W          E
♣ ---                    S
```

West	North	East	South
1♡	Pass	1NT	2♠
4♡	4♠	Double	All pass

West leads the ♡A: five – three – seven.

What do you play at trick 2?

24. Pairs: Dealer West : East-West vulnerable

Contract: 4♠ doubled
Lead: ♡A

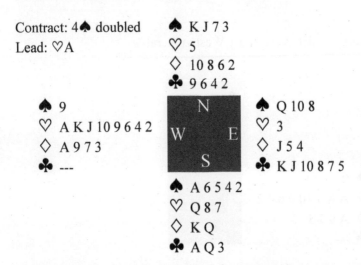

♠ K J 7 3
♡ 5
◇ 10 8 6 2
♣ 9 6 4 2

♠ 9
♡ A K J 10 9 6 4 2
◇ A 9 7 3
♣ ---

♠ Q 10 8
♡ 3
◇ J 5 4
♣ K J 10 8 7 5

♠ A 6 5 4 2
♡ Q 8 7
◇ K Q
♣ A Q 3

West did well not to remove East's double of 4♠ to 5♡. That fails on normal lines. West also did well not to lead ♡2 in the hope that East might win and return a club. That allows 4♠ to make.

There is a good chance that East began with a singleton heart and, given the double, is hoping to score at least one heart ruff. West should play ♡2 at trick 2. If the missing hearts were 2-2 initially and South has the ♡Q, one discard from dummy will be of little use to South. Indeed, South will probably ruff in dummy anyway.

On the actual layout, if declarer ruffs the second heart with the ♠K, East has two trump tricks. If declarer ruffs at trick 2 with a lower trump, East over-ruffs as cheaply as possible. East now switches to the ♣J: queen – ♠9 – ♣2. Now the ♡K from West promotes a trump trick for East. After this defence, declarer figures to lose two spades with East, the ♡A, a club ruff with West, the ◇A and a club trick for East later.

My bridge partner said he needed more space, so I locked him out of the bridge club.

25. Teams: Dealer North : Both vulnerable

                 ♠ 10 7 5 2
                 ♡ 10 3
                 ◇ A K Q J 4
                 ♣ 10 5

♠ A 6
♡ 9 8 7 5 2   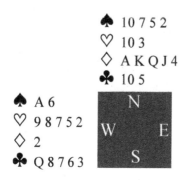
◇ 2
♣ Q 8 7 6 3

West	North	East	South
	Pass	1♡	1♠
4♡	4♠	All pass	

West leads the ◇2: ace – three – six.
Declarer plays the ♠2: eight – king – ace.
How would you continue as West?

25. Teams: Dealer North : Both vulnerable

Contract: 4 ♠
Lead: ◇2

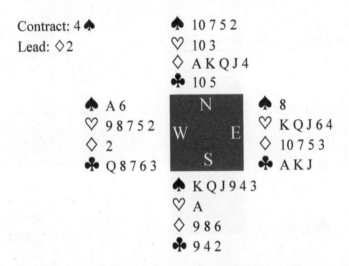

After the ◇2 lead to the ◇A and a trump to the king and ace, the natural inclination for West is to play a heart. After all that is the suit which partner bid. A heart switch will be fatal for the defence. South wins, draws West's remaining trump and runs the diamonds to make eleven tricks.

West needs to note East's play at trick 1. A diamond continuation is futile and, accordingly, an attitude signal or a count signal is not suitable for this situation. East can read West's lead as a singleton and should give a suit-preference signal at trick 1. East's ◇3, the lowest diamonds, asks for the lowest suit, clubs. West should switch to a club, preferably the ♣8 to deny interest in a club return. East wins with the ♣K, gives West a diamond ruff and the next club defeats 4♠.

When it is clear that continuing the suit led is pointless, then a suit-preference signal is appropriate.

Extremely rare dish for bridge players: Humble pie.

26. Teams: Dealer East : Both vulnerable

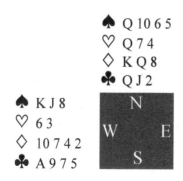

♠ Q 10 6 5
♡ Q 7 4
♢ K Q 8
♣ Q J 2

♠ K J 8
♡ 6 3
♢ 10 7 4 2
♣ A 9 7 5

West	North	East	South
		Pass	1♡
Pass	1♠	Pass	2♡
Pass	4♡	All pass	

West leads the ♢2 (fourth-highest): king – three – six.
Declarer plays the ♢8, East the ♢A and South the ♢J.
Which diamond would you play as West?

26. Teams: Dealer East : Both vulnerable

Contract: 4♡
Lead: ◇2

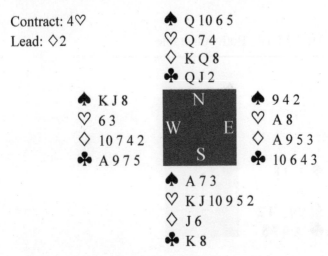

```
              ♠ Q 10 6 5
              ♡ Q 7 4
              ◇ K Q 8
              ♣ Q J 2
  ♠ K J 8                    ♠ 9 4 2
  ♡ 6 3          N           ♡ A 8
  ◇ 10 7 4 2  W     E        ◇ A 9 5 3
  ♣ A 9 7 5      S           ♣ 10 6 4 3
              ♠ A 7 3
              ♡ K J 10 9 5 2
              ◇ J 6
              ♣ K 8
```

From West's ◇2 (fourth-highest), East knew West began with 3-4 diamonds and so South had at least two diamonds. East therefore could afford to duck at trick 1 and take the ◇A on the second diamond. East's problem now is whether to switch to spades or to clubs. A club switch would be fatal, as would a third diamond or a trump. Declarer plays the ♣K and knocks out the ♣A. Declarer can reach dummy on the third round of hearts and discard two spades, one on the third diamond and one on the third club.

East needs to switch to a spade at trick 3. How can East tell? West needs to help. On the ◇A at trick 2, West should play the ◇10 as a suit-preference signal, high card for the high suit, spades. East should shift to the ♠9, high to deny interest in a spade return.

If South had ♠K-J and ♣A-x-x, a club shift would be needed. In that case, with the ♠A and the ♣K, West would play the ◇4 on the ◇A, low card to ask for the low suit, trumps excluded.

Flounder: noun: a fish; verb: how our partners usually perform during a bridge session.

27. Pairs: Dealer West : Both vulnerable

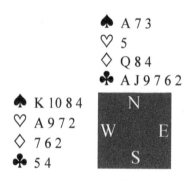

♠ A 7 3
♡ 5
♢ Q 8 4
♣ A J 9 7 6 2

♠ K 10 8 4
♡ A 9 7 2
♢ 7 6 2
♣ 5 4

West	North	East	South
Pass	Pass	1NT (1)	Pass
Pass	2♣ (2)	Pass	2♢ (3)
Double (4)	Pass	Pass	Pass

(1) 15-17 points
(2) Clubs and another suit
(3) Pass or correct
(4) For takeout

West leads the ♢7: four – ten – jack.
South plays the ♣10: five – two – queen.
East cashes the ♢K, ♢A.
East switches to the ♡3: eight – nine – five.
What would you do now as West?

27. Pairs: Dealer West : Both vulnerable

Contract: 2◇ doubled
Lead: ◇7:

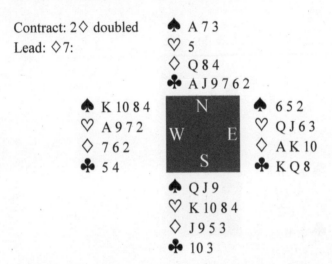

♠ A 7 3
♡ 5
◇ Q 8 4
♣ A J 9 7 6 2

♠ K 10 8 4
♡ A 9 7 2
◇ 7 6 2
♣ 5 4

♠ 6 5 2
♡ Q J 6 3
◇ A K 10
♣ K Q 8

♠ Q J 9
♡ K 10 8 4
◇ J 9 5 3
♣ 10 3

The North hand does not quite tally with 2♣ as clubs and another. Maybe it was a misunderstanding about 2♣ in the balancing seat.

Declarer is threatening to set up the clubs via ♣A and a club ruff, with the ♠A as entry. To counter that, West needs to dislodge dummy's ♠A. A low spade will work if East has the ♠Q, but that is not likely. East has shown up with ◇A-K, presumably ♣K-Q and, from the ♡3 (low-like), some values in hearts. In any event, you need not rely on partner to hold the ♠Q. Simply switch to the ♠K yourself. If partner does have the ♠Q, so much the better.

If declarer captures the ♠K, the club suit is dead (unless South began with three clubs). If declarer ducks, you can cash the ♡A and make six tricks for +200 and an excellent match-point score.

South could have succeeded by playing the ♡10, not the ♡8, and East could have ensured defeated by switching to ♡Q, not ♡3.

Some can be destroyed by defeat and some are made small and mean by victory.

28. Teams: Dealer East : Both vulnerable

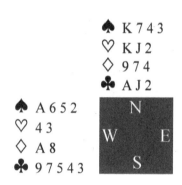

♠ K 7 4 3
♡ K J 2
◇ 9 7 4
♣ A J 2

♠ A 6 5 2
♡ 4 3
◇ A 8
♣ 9 7 5 4 3

West	North	East	South
		Pass	1♡ (1)
Pass	1♠	Pass	1NT (2)
Pass	2♣ (3)	Pass	2◇
Pass	3♡ (4)	Pass	4♡
Pass	Pass	Pass	

(1) Playing 5-card majors
(2) 11-14 points
(3) Forces opener to bid 2◇
(4) A strong invitation to game in hearts

West leads the ◇A: four – five (low-like / high-hate) – ten.
West continues with the ◇8: seven – queen – jack.
At trick 3 East plays the ◇K: ◇3 from South . . .
What card should West play?

28. Teams: Dealer East : Both vulnerable

Contract: 4♡
Lead: ◇A

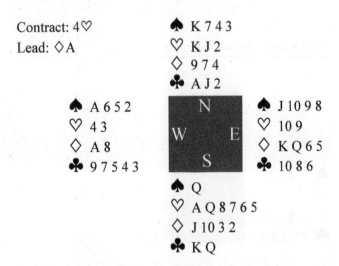

Dummy (North):
♠ K 7 4 3
♡ K J 2
◇ 9 7 4
♣ A J 2

West:
♠ A 6 5 2
♡ 4 3
◇ A 8
♣ 9 7 5 4 3

East:
♠ J 10 9 8
♡ 10 9
◇ K Q 6 5
♣ 10 8 6

South:
♠ Q
♡ A Q 8 7 6 5
◇ J 10 3 2
♣ K Q

You do not like South's bidding? Neither do I. It is not textbook, but it is a free country. Any complaint about South's bidding will not excuse you if you fail to defeat the contract.

After the defence takes the first three tricks, it is vital that the ♠A is cashed at trick 4, else South can draw trumps and pitch the ♠Q on the third club winner in dummy.

East-West might have excellent signalling methods, but no matter how clear the signal, it is always possible for partner not to see it or to misinterpret it or to ignore it. West should not rely on East to play a spade. Instead, West should ruff the ◇K at trick 3 and play the ♠A. Then partner cannot get it wrong.

Ask not what your partner can do for you.
Ask what you can do yourself.

29. Teams: Dealer East : Both vulnerable

♠ K 7 4 3
♡ K J 2
◇ 9 7 4
♣ A J 2

♠ Q 6 5 2
♡ Q 3
◇ A 8
♣ 9 7 5 4 3

West	North	East	South
		Pass	1♡ (1)
Pass	1♠	Pass	1NT (2)
Pass	2♣ (3)	Pass	2◇
Pass	3♡ (4)	Pass	4♡
Pass	Pass	Pass	

(1) Playing 5-card majors
(2) 11-14 points
(3) Forces opener to bid 2◇
(4) A strong invitation to game in hearts

West leads the ◇A: four – two (low-like) – ten.
West continues with the ◇8: seven – queen – jack.
At trick 3 East plays the ◇K: ◇3 from South . . .
What card should West play?

29. Teams: Dealer North : Both vulnerable

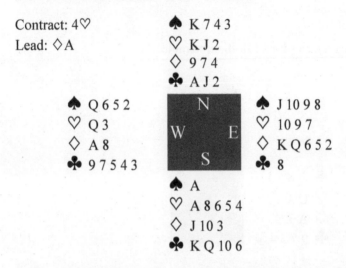

Contract: 4♡
Lead: ◇A

♠ K 7 4 3
♡ K J 2
◇ 9 7 4
♣ A J 2

♠ Q 6 5 2
♡ Q 3
◇ A 8
♣ 9 7 5 4 3

♠ J 10 9 8
♡ 10 9 7
◇ K Q 6 5 2
♣ 8

♠ A
♡ A 8 6 5 4
◇ J 10 3
♣ K Q 10 6

Did you think you are experiencing *déja vu* after Puzzle 28? Similar situation, but quite a different solution.

Your side has taken three tricks. You have 8 HCP, dummy has 12. To accept the invitation, South figures to have 14 HCP. That leaves partner with about 5-6 HCP at best. As partner has already shown up with 5 HCP, partner will not have the ♠A or ♣K.

Your best chance for an extra trick is in the trump suit. You should signal for a diamond continuation. Playing McKenny suit-preference signals, the ♣3 discard says, 'Don't play a club. Play the lower of the other suits.' Using odd-even discards, the ♣4 carries the same message.

If East plays a spade, a club or a trump, South succeeds routinely. If East continues diamonds, West can force out a trump honour from dummy, no matter what South does. East then comes to a trump trick. Only one pair in the 2002 Cavendish defeated 4♡.

Every bridge player can be a fool on one board a session. Competence consists in not exceeding that.

30. Teams: Dealer East : Both vulnerable

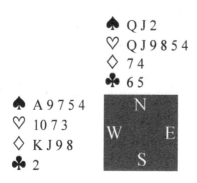

♠ Q J 2
♥ Q J 9 8 5 4
♦ 7 4
♣ 6 5

♠ A 9 7 5 4
♥ 10 7 3
♦ K J 9 8
♣ 2

West	North	East	South
		1♣	1NT (1)
Pass	2◇ (2)	3♣	3♡ (3)
Pass	4♡	Pass	Pass
Double	Pass	Pass	Pass

(1) 15-18 points
(2) Transfer to hearts
(3) Maximum 1NT with 4-5 hearts

West leads the ♣2: five – ace – three.
East continues with the ♣K: seven from South.
What card should West play?

30. Teams: Dealer East : Both vulnerable

Contract: 4♡ doubled
Lead: ♣2

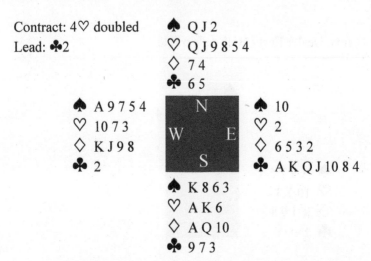

♠ Q J 2
♡ Q J 9 8 5 4
◇ 7 4
♣ 6 5

♠ A 9 7 5 4   ♠ 10
♡ 10 7 3   ♡ 2
◇ K J 9 8   ◇ 6 5 3 2
♣ 2   ♣ A K Q J 10 8 4

♠ K 8 6 3
♡ A K 6
◇ A Q 10
♣ 9 7 3

East's ♣A then ♣K was abnormal. A defender usually wins with the cheapest of equally high cards. West should read ♣A then ♣K as suit preference for spades and play East for ♠K-x or a spade singleton. Therefore, West should signal for a spade switch (♠9 for standard discards or odd-encouraging, ♠2 if playing reverse attitude). After ♠10 to ♠A and a spade ruff, East-West +200.

The problem is South is only one down. If East shifts to a diamond at trick 3, declarer might finesse ◇Q in the hope of making 4♡. West wins and now ♠A and a spade ruff = two down, +500.

West might be concerned that South has the ♣Q for a diamond discard from dummy. How can East help West? East might have played ♣A and ♣Q / ♣J at trick 2 for the same message. If South did have a club winner, East would play a third club for West to ruff. As long as West knows that South has no club winner for a diamond discard, West can safely signal for a diamond switch.

Never let partner's signals interfere with doing the right thing.

31. Teams: Dealer North : Nil vulnerable

♠ A J 8 4
♡ Q 10 5 3
◇ Q 7 3
♣ 10 2

♠ K 10 5
♡ 8 7 6
◇ A 10 2
♣ A 7 5 3

West	North	East	South
	Pass	Pass	2♡ (1)
Pass	3♡ (2)	All pass	

(1) Weak two, five or six hearts
(2) Not invitational

1. West leads the ♡8: three – king – ace.
2. South plays the ♣Q: three – two – king.
3. East returns the ♣J: ♡2 – ♣5 – ♣10.
4. South plays the ♡J: seven – five – ♣4
5. And the ♠2: five – jack – seven (reverse count)
6. And the ♡Q: ♣8 – ♡4 – ♡6
7. And the ♠4: three – queen – king.

What should West do now?

31. Teams: Dealer North : Nil vulnerable

Contract: 3♡
Lead: ♡8

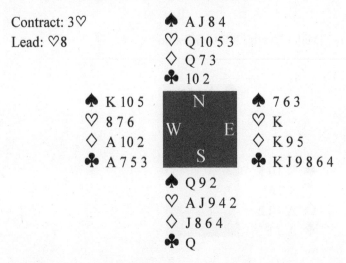

♠ A J 8 4
♡ Q 10 5 3
◇ Q 7 3
♣ 10 2

♠ K 10 5
♡ 8 7 6
◇ A 10 2
♣ A 7 5 3

♠ 7 6 3
♡ K
◇ K 9 5
♣ K J 9 8 6 4

♠ Q 9 2
♡ A J 9 4 2
◇ J 8 6 4
♣ Q

If West is not focused after trick 7 or has not been paying attention, West might shift to the ◇A and a second diamond, hoping East began with K-J-x in diamonds. That will allow South to make 3♡, losing a spade, a club and only two diamonds.

After trick 1, West can place South with five hearts, not six. When South ruffs the club return at trick 3, South began with only one club. South is unlikely to open 2♡ with four spades and five hearts and this is confirmed by East's play in spades, ♠7 then ♠3, reverse count, showing an odd number of spades, clearly three.

South has shown up with the ♠Q, ♡A-J, ♣Q, 9 HCP. The ◇K will be with East, else South has 12 HCP and would open 1♡.

As South's hand pattern is known to be 3-5-4-1, West should return a spade. A diamond discard on the thirteenth spade will not help South. On the actual layout, no matter how South continues, East-West can come to three diamond tricks to defeat 3♡.

Three tips for success at bridge: Focus, focus, focus.

32. Teams: Dealer North : Both vulnerable

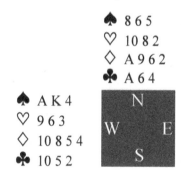

♠ 8 6 5
♡ 10 8 2
♢ A 9 6 2
♣ A 6 4

♠ A K 4
♡ 9 6 3
♢ 10 8 5 4
♣ 10 5 2

West	North	East	South
	Pass	1♣	Double
1♢	1NT	3♣	3♠
Pass	4♠	All pass	

West leads the ♣2: ace – three – ♡4.
Declarer plays dummy's ♠5: two – queen . . .
Plan the defence.

32. Teams: Dealer North : Both vulnerable

Contract: 4♠
Lead: ♣2

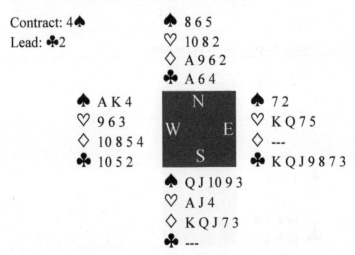

Firstly, there is no point ducking the ♠Q. Declarer can either abandon trumps with six trumps or play another trump if 3♠ was based on a 5-card suit.

Secondly, there is no rush to attack hearts just because declarer discarded one. If declarer has any heart losers, they are not going anywhere. Dummy will not provide any more discards for South.

Thirdly, what did you make of partner's ♣3 at trick 1. East knew that your ♣2 was either a singleton or bottom from 10-5-2. If a singleton, East's ♣3 was suit-preference to East's potential entry. If the ♣2 was from a 3-card holding, then South had no clubs. Likewise, the ♣3 was suit-preference for diamonds, as a club continuation would be pointless.

West should take the ♠Q with the ♠K and switch to a diamond. East ruffs. South loses two spades, a heart and the diamond ruff.

Sometimes you need partner's signal. At other times you can manage without.

33. Teams: Dealer East : North-South vulnerable

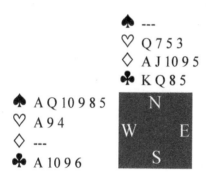

♠ ---
♡ Q 7 5 3
◇ A J 10 9 5
♣ K Q 8 5

♠ A Q 10 9 8 5
♡ A 9 4
◇ ---
♣ A 10 9 6

West	North	East	South
		Pass	1◇ (1)
Double	2NT (2)	Pass	3◇ (3)
3♠	5◇	Pass	Pass
Double	Pass	Pass	Pass

(1) 10-14 points, 4+ diamonds
(2) Strong diamond raise
(3) Minimum opening

West leads the ♠A: ◇5 – ♠6 – ♠4.
Declarer plays the ◇9: four – king – ♠5
And the ♠7: eight – ◇10 – ♠2.
Next comes the ♣5: two – jack – ace.

What should West play at trick 5?

33. Teams: Dealer East : North-South vulnerable

Contract: 5 ◇ doubled
Lead: ♠A

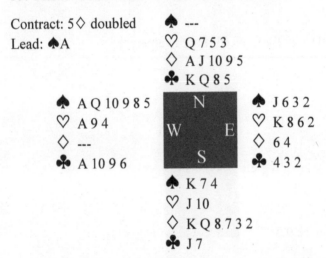

♠ ---
♡ Q 7 5 3
◇ A J 10 9 5
♣ K Q 8 5

♠ A Q 10 9 8 5
♡ A 9 4
◇ ---
♣ A 10 9 6

♠ J 6 3 2
♡ K 8 6 2
◇ 6 4
♣ 4 3 2

♠ K 7 4
♡ J 10
◇ K Q 8 7 3 2
♣ J 7

You have no spade tricks coming and almost certainly no club tricks. If partner has a trump trick, that will be lucky. Ask yourself, where can you find two more tricks to defeat 5 ◇?

Note East's carding. East's ♠2 at trick 3 = an initial holding of four spades. East's ♣2, lowest, showed three clubs. You can place South with three spades and two clubs. If South is 3-3-5-2 or 3-2-6-2, including the ♡K, you cannot score more than one club and one heart trick.

All of this means that you need East to have the ♡K and so you must switch to the ♡A at trick 5. That will be one down if East has the ♡K and two down if East also has a trump trick. In an international match, West returned a club at trick 5. Declarer took the ♣K, drew East's second trump with the ◇A and the ♣Q allowed South to pitch a heart loser and make eleven tricks. East-West were minus-750 instead of plus-200.

Hell hath no fury like a bridge partner whose signals are scorned.

34. Rubber bridge: Dealer West : East-West vulnerable

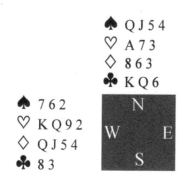

```
                    ♠ Q J 5 4
                    ♡ A 7 3
                    ♢ 8 6 3
                    ♣ K Q 6
  ♠ 7 6 2
  ♡ K Q 9 2
  ♢ Q J 5 4
  ♣ 8 3
```

West	North	East	South
Pass	1♠	Pass	2NT (1)
Pass	3NT	All pass	

(1) Natural, 13-15 points, balanced, forcing to game

West leads ♡2: three – ten – five.
East returns the ♡J: six from South . . .

What is the heart position? What do you play at trick 2?

Whatever card you play, declarer will play dummy's ♡7. Suppose you cover the ♡J with the ♡Q, winning. What do you play next?

34. Rubber bridge: Dealer West : East-West vulnerable

Contract: 3NT
Lead: ♡2

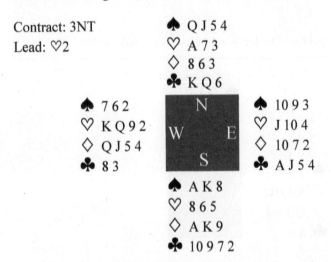

♠ Q J 5 4
♡ A 7 3
◊ 8 6 3
♣ K Q 6

♠ 7 6 2
♡ K Q 9 2
◊ Q J 5 4
♣ 8 3

♠ 10 9 3
♡ J 10 4
◊ 10 7 2
♣ A J 5 4

♠ A K 8
♡ 8 6 5
◊ A K 9
♣ 10 9 7 2

East won trick 1 with ♡10 and returned ♡J. With four hearts, East would have returned the lowest heart. The ♡J at trick 2 is either from J-10 or J-10-x.

West should overtake ♡J with ♡Q. Declarer needs to duck this, else the defence can come to three heart tricks. Playing a third heart is futile. West has no quick entry to enjoy the last heart. If you let East's ♡J win, East might continue with a third heart.

West should switch to ◊Q at trick 3. As East has the ◊10, a low diamond works, but the ◊Q caters for ◊A-K-10 with declarer. South takes ◊A and plays ♣2: eight – king – ace. East returns a diamond. The defence takes two hearts, a diamond and two clubs.

If West continues with a heart at trick 3, South can set up two club tricks and make four spades, one heart, two diamonds and two clubs before the defence can come to a fifth trick.

If declarer had not gone one down, he would have made it.

35. Teams: Dealer South : Nil vulnerable

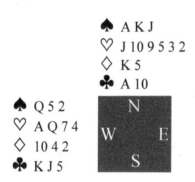

♠ A K J
♡ J 10 9 5 3 2
◇ K 5
♣ A 10

♠ Q 5 2
♡ A Q 7 4
◇ 10 4 2
♣ K J 5

West	North	East	South
			Pass
1NT (1)	Double	Redouble (2)	Pass
2♣	2♡	Pass	3NT
Pass	Pass	Pass	

(1) 12-14 points, balanced shape
(2) Rescue; asks opener to bid 2♣, but does not promise a club suit

West leads ♣K: ace – nine (reverse attitude, discouraging) – two.
Declarer plays dummy's HJ: six – eight – queen.
What next for West?

35. Teams: Dealer South : Nil vulnerable

Contract: 3NT
Lead: ♣K

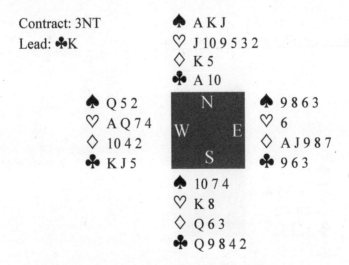

♠ A K J
♡ J 10 9 5 3 2
♢ K 5
♣ A 10

♠ Q 5 2
♡ A Q 7 4
♢ 10 4 2
♣ K J 5

♠ 9 8 6 3
♡ 6
♢ A J 9 8 7
♣ 9 6 3

♠ 10 7 4
♡ K 8
♢ Q 6 3
♣ Q 9 8 4 2

North-South did well to avoid 4♡. The defence can come to a club, a diamond and two heart tricks against 4♡.

East's rescue of 1NT doubled was *en route* to 2♢ but, unaware of this, West led ♣K. Declarer took ♣A. East's ♣9 was 'high-hate'.

Since East cannot want spades or hearts and has discouraged clubs, West should deduce that East is interested in diamonds. West should switch to a diamond. On the actual layout, it does not matter which diamond West chooses, but from 10-x-x the bottom card is normal, unless there is a powerful reason to choose the ten.

If West shifts to a diamond, South has no successful play. If declarer plays dummy's ♢K, East wins and plays a second diamond. South needs to duck and East wins. With no entry to the diamonds even if established, East then needs to revert to clubs to set up West's ♣J to defeat the contract.

My partner is a nobody, and nobody is a perfect bridge player. Therefore, my partner is a perfect bridge player.

36. Teams: Dealer East : Both vulnerable

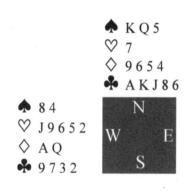

♠ K Q 5
♡ 7
♢ 9 6 5 4
♣ A K J 8 6

♠ 8 4
♡ J 9 6 5 2
♢ A Q
♣ 9 7 3 2

West	North	East	South
		1♡	1♠
4♡	4♠	All pass	

West leads the ♡5 and East wins with the ♡Q.
East shifts to the ♢2. South plays the ♢3.
Plan West's defence.

36. Teams: Dealer East : Both vulnerable

Contract: 4♠
Lead: ♡5

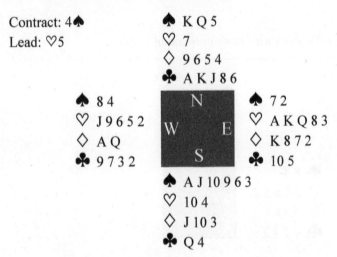

```
                    ♠ K Q 5
                    ♡ 7
                    ◇ 9 6 5 4
                    ♣ A K J 8 6
    ♠ 8 4            N          ♠ 7 2
    ♡ J 9 6 5 2              ♡ A K Q 8 3
    ◇ A Q       W       E    ◇ K 8 7 2
    ♣ 9 7 3 2        S        ♣ 10 5
                    ♠ A J 10 9 6 3
                    ♡ 10 4
                    ◇ J 10 3
                    ♣ Q 4
```

After ♡5, won by the ♡Q, and East shifts to the ◇2, South playing the ◇3, it is essential that West takes time out and does not proceed on 'automatic pilot'.

South figures to have 5+ spades, headed by ♠A. That means the defence cannot score any spade tricks. You cannot expect any club tricks for the defence, whether East has ♣Q, ♣Q-x or ♣Q-x-x.

The only hope is for three tricks from the diamonds. That requires East to have the ◇K. That is a reasonable expectation from East's switch to the ◇2: lowest card switch = low-like for diamonds.

Beware of the mechanical play of winning trick 2 with the ◇Q. If you do, the defence is dead. You must win with the ◇A and return the ◇Q. East needs to overtake with the ◇K and play a third diamond. You ruff and 4♠ is one down.

If calmness and serenity are your desires in life, perhaps bridge is not for you.

37. Teams: Dealer North : Nil vulnerable

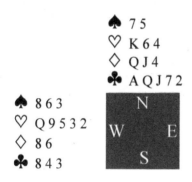

♠ 7 5
♡ K 6 4
◇ Q J 4
♣ A Q J 7 2

♠ 8 6 3
♡ Q 9 5 3 2
◇ 8 6
♣ 8 4 3

West	North	East	South
	1♣	1◇	1♠
Pass	1NT	Pass	4♠
Pass	Pass	Pass	

West leads the ◇8: queen – ace – two .
East returns the ◇3: five – six – jack.
Declarer plays the ♠5 from dummy and captures East's ♠Q.
South continues with the ♠9.

How have you planned the defence so far?

Suppose partner captures the ♠9 with the ♠K and returns the ◇7:
king from South and you ruff. What next?

37. Teams: Dealer North : Nil vulnerable

Contract: 4♠
Lead: ◇8

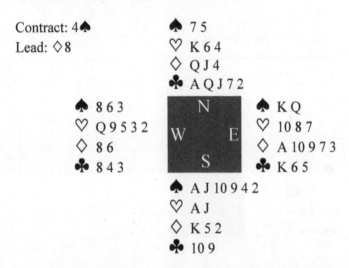

♠ 7 5
♡ K 6 4
◇ Q J 4
♣ A Q J 7 2

♠ 8 6 3
♡ Q 9 5 3 2
◇ 8 6
♣ 8 4 3

♠ K Q
♡ 10 8 7
◇ A 10 9 7 3
♣ K 6 5

♠ A J 10 9 4 2
♡ A J
◇ K 5 2
♣ 10 9

From West's ◇8 and ◇6, East knows West began with a
doubleton diamond. East needs to know whether West can ruff the
third diamond. South's jump to 4♠ might be based on six spades
or seven spades. To confirm holding three trumps, West should
follow to tricks 3 and 4 with the ♠6 and the ♠3. High-low in
trumps show an odd number of trumps, here clearly three.

When West does ruff the third diamond, West should switch to a
club, despite dummy having such strong clubs. East has asked for
a club with the ◇3 (lowest diamond for the lowest suit) at trick 2
in case the ◇8 lead was a singleton. At trick 5, when East played
the ◇7 for West to ruff, that was also East's lowest diamond as
suit-preference for clubs.

A club return at trick 6 will defeat 4♠. Note that a heart return at
trick 6 would allow South to make 4♠. South wins with the ♡J,
cashes ♡A, crosses to ♣A and discards the club loser on the ♡K.

  *'You gotta trust partner', they say, despite all your previous
experiences.*

38. Teams: Dealer North : Nil vulnerable

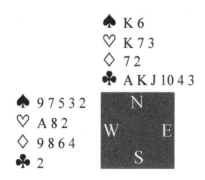

♠ K 6
♡ K 7 3
◇ 7 2
♣ A K J 10 4 3

♠ 9 7 5 3 2
♡ A 8 2
◇ 9 8 6 4
♣ 2

West	North	East	South
	1♣	Pass	1♡
Pass	2♣	Pass	2NT
Pass	3NT	All pass	

West leads the ♠3: king – ace – four.
East continues with the ♠J and ♠Q, South following with the ♠8 and the ♠10.

How should West plan the defence?

38. Teams: Dealer North : Nil vulnerable

Contract: 3NT
Lead: ♠3

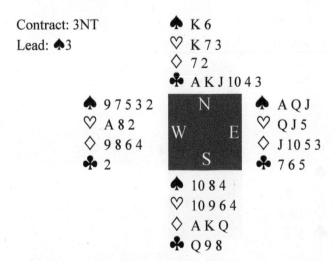

                         ♠ K 6
                         ♡ K 7 3
                         ♢ 7 2
                         ♣ A K J 10 4 3

♠ 9 7 5 3 2   ♠ A Q J
♡ A 8 2   ♡ Q J 5
♢ 9 8 6 4   ♢ J 10 5 3
♣ 2   ♣ 7 6 5

                         ♠ 10 8 4
                         ♡ 10 9 6 4
                         ♢ A K Q
                         ♣ Q 9 8

The defence has taken the first three tricks and now West has two more spade winners, plus the ♡A as entry to take 3NT two down. You know that, but does partner know where your entry lies? Looking at dummy's clubs and knowing South bid hearts, what will be East's natural inclination at trick 4? Sure, a diamond shift.

To put partner on the right track, West should follow with the ♠9 on trick 2 and the ♠7 on trick 3, the highest card each time to ask partner to play the highest suit (outside spades). If partner shifts to a heart, you will be all smiles as you beat the contract by two tricks. If East switches to a diamond, declarer has nine tricks via three diamonds and six clubs.

This is another instance where you must watch out for 'automatic pilot' in following low on the second and third spade.

Bridge players do it with signals to their partner.

39. Teams: Dealer West : North-South vulnerable

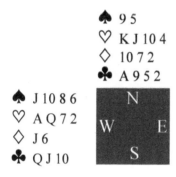

```
                    ♠ 9 5
                    ♡ K J 10 4
                    ◇ 10 7 2
                    ♣ A 9 5 2
    ♠ J 10 8 6           N
    ♡ A Q 7 2
    ◇ J 6           W        E
    ♣ Q J 10           S
```

West	North	East	South
Pass	Pass	Pass	1◇
Double	1♡	1♠	1NT
2♠	Double (1)	Pass	3◇
Pass	Pass	Pass	

(1) For takeout

West leads the ♠J: five – ace – four.
East switches to the ♡5: ♡6 from South.
Plan the defence for West.

39. Teams: Dealer West : North-South vulnerable

Contract: 3♦
Lead: ♠J

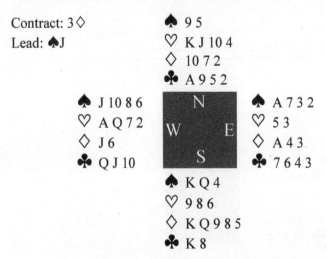

```
              ♠ 9 5
              ♡ K J 10 4
              ◇ 10 7 2
              ♣ A 9 5 2
♠ J 10 8 6          N          ♠ A 7 3 2
♡ A Q 7 2                       ♡ 5 3
◇ J 6        W         E        ◇ A 4 3
♣ Q J 10          S            ♣ 7 6 4 3
              ♠ K Q 4
              ♡ 9 8 6
              ◇ K Q 9 8 5
              ♣ K 8
```

West should encourage hearts with the ♡7 (standard signalling) or
the ♡2 (reverse attitude). When East comes in with the ◇A later,
East continues with the ♡3. Now West takes the ♡A and gives
East a heart ruff. That holds declarer to nine tricks and you are –
110. As your North-South team-mates at the other table made
+130 in 3◇, this simple defence wins 1 Imp. Every Imp can be
vital. Datum (average) on the deal was North-South +110.

At the table, West took the ♡A at trick 2 and the heart ruff
vanished. No swing. East will not have a singleton heart. That
would give South four hearts and, with such support, South would
have raised to 2♡ rather than rebid 1NT.

Have you ever seen the look on partner's face when you find a
brilliant card in defence, the only card to shoot the contract? No,
me neither.

40. Teams: Dealer North : Both vulnerable

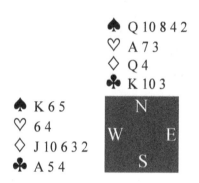

```
              ♠ Q 10 8 4 2
              ♡ A 7 3
              ◇ Q 4
              ♣ K 10 3
  ♠ K 6 5            N
  ♡ 6 4
  ◇ J 10 6 3 2    W     E
  ♣ A 5 4            S
```

West	North	East	South
	1♠	Pass	2♡
Pass	4♡ (1)	All pass	

(1) Minimum opening. 3♡ would have shown a strong opening hand.

1. West leads the ◇3: four – ace – seven.
2. East returns the ◇9: eight – two – queen.
3. South plays dummy's ♡A: five – two – four.
4. South plays the ♡3 from dummy: eight – king – six.
5. South continues with the ♡Q: ◇6 – ♡7 – ♡9.
6. South plays the ♠3: five – ten – jack.
7. East switches to the ♣Q: two – ace – three.

What should West play at trick 8?

40. Teams: Dealer North : Both vulnerable

Contract: 4♡
Lead: ◇3

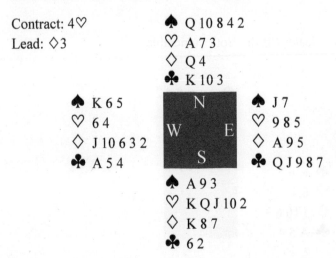

♠ Q 10 8 4 2
♡ A 7 3
◇ Q 4
♣ K 10 3

♠ K 6 5
♡ 6 4
◇ J 10 6 3 2
♣ A 5 4

♠ J 7
♡ 9 8 5
◇ A 9 5
♣ Q J 9 8 7

♠ A 9 3
♡ K Q J 10 2
◇ K 8 7
♣ 6 2

South's 2♡ showed 5+ hearts and, from the early play, you know that South has exactly five hearts. From East's return of the ◇9 at trick 2, East will have started with ◇A-9 doubleton or ◇A-9-x. That gives South three or four diamonds. If South has one club, South must have three or four spades. Since East took the ♠8 with the ♠J, South is known to hold the ♠9.

West's safest play at trick 8 is a club, as East would not switch to the ♣Q without the ♣J as well. A diamond exit is safe, too.

You (and I) would think this problem is trivial, except that, in the final of a National Teams, West played the ♠K at trick 8??? There was nowhere for declarer to park a spade loser and so there was no urgency to play a spade. South now made ten tricks for +620. East-West were thus −10 Imps instead of +7 (North-South were +170 at the other table after they bid Pass : 1♡, 1♠, all pass).

Bridge is 90% mental and 10% being mental.

41. Teams: Dealer North : North-South vulnerable

♠ A 8 5 2
♡ J 8 7 2
◇ J 7
♣ Q 10 2

♠ 9 3
♡ K Q 10 6 4
◇ 8 5
♣ K 8 7 6

West	North	East	South
	Pass	2♡ (1)	2♠
Pass	3♠	Pass	4♠
Pass	Pass	Pass	

(1) Weak, 5 hearts and a 4+ minor

West leads the ♡9: jack – queen – ace.
South plays the ♠4: ten – ace – three.
South continues with the ♠2: nine – king – queen.
South plays the ◇4: king – seven – five.
West returns the ♡3: two – six – five.
What do you do now as East?

41. Teams: Dealer North : North-South vulnerable

Contract: 4♠
Lead: ♡9

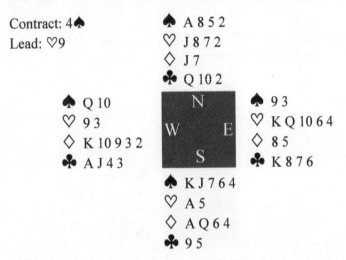

                    ♠ A 8 5 2
                    ♡ J 8 7 2
                    ♢ J 7
                    ♣ Q 10 2

♠ Q 10   ♠ 9 3
♡ 9 3   ♡ K Q 10 6 4
♢ K 10 9 3 2   ♢ 8 5
♣ A J 4 3   ♣ K 8 7 6

                    ♠ K J 7 6 4
                    ♡ A 5
                    ♢ A Q 6 4
                    ♣ 9 5

From trick 1, ♡9: jack – queen – ace, South deduced that East had
♡K-Q in hearts and also a top club, as West would lead a top club
with clubs headed by A-K. As that gave East 8 or 9 HCP, South
placed the ♢K with West and played the ♢4 at trick 4.

West rose with ♢K and returned ♡3. To give East a chance to err,
South played dummy's ♡2 and East won with the ♡6. South was
hoping East would continue hearts. South could ruff, play ♢6 to
♢J, ruff a heart and discard two clubs from dummy on ♢A, ♢Q.

After the ♡6 wins, a club shift is needed. With ♢A-K, West
would lead ♢A initially. With ♢K-Q, West would win with ♢Q,
not ♢K. As East can place South with ♢A + ♢Q, the risk of club
discards from dummy on South's winning diamonds is now clear.

If South has ♣A, the defence will probably not score any more
tricks. East does best to switch to ♣K. This is to make sure that
West does not do the wrong thing if East switches to a low club.

'Unlucky break: An opponent held all eight missing trumps.'

42. Teams: Dealer South : Nil vulnerable

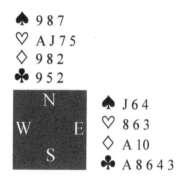

```
            ♠ 9 8 7
            ♡ A J 7 5
            ◇ 9 8 2
            ♣ 9 5 2
         N              ♠ J 6 4
      W     E           ♡ 8 6 3
         S              ◇ A 10
                        ♣ A 8 6 4 3
```

West	North	East	South
			1♡
3◇ (1)	Pass	Pass	Double (2)
Pass	4♡	All pass	

(1) Weak jump-overcall, 6+ diamonds, 6-10 points
(2) For takeout

West leads the ◇K: two – ten – seven.
West switches to the ♣K: two – three (low-encouraging) – ten.
West continues with the ♣Q: five from dummy . . .
How will you defend as East?

If you overtake ♣Q with the ♣A, South plays the ♣J. What next?

42. Teams: Dealer South : Nil vulnerable

Contract: 4♡
Lead: ◇K

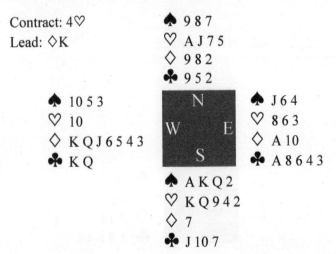

```
                    ♠ 9 8 7
                    ♡ A J 7 5
                    ◇ 9 8 2
                    ♣ 9 5 2
    ♠ 10 5 3                        ♠ J 6 4
    ♡ 10                            ♡ 8 6 3
    ◇ K Q J 6 5 4 3                 ◇ A 10
    ♣ K Q                           ♣ A 8 6 4 3
                    ♠ A K Q 2
                    ♡ K Q 9 4 2
                    ◇ 7
                    ♣ J 10 7
```

Recognizing that a second diamond would be futile, West shifted to the ♣K, followed by the ♣Q. East should overtake the ♣Q with the ♣A and return a club. West ruffs and 4♡ is one down.

South should make it tough for East by dropping the ♣10 on the first club and the ♣J on the next club. South is trying to create an illusion of holding the ♣J-10 doubleton. If East is fooled into believing that, East will probably be tempted to play the ◇A. South ruffs, draws trumps and plays spades, discarding a club from dummy on the ♠2 when the spades behave.

If a second diamond trick were available, West could have played a diamond at trick 2 (the ◇3 as suit-preference for clubs). As West switched at trick 2, there is a strong inference that there was no second diamond trick for the defence. Therefore, East should play a third club.

Reverse signal: Partner takes the signal to mean the opposite of what you intended.

43. Teams: Dealer North : Nil vulnerable

<pre>
                ♠ K 7 3 2
                ♡ K Q 10 7 6 5
                ◇ K J
                ♣ 10
                             ♠ 10 5
                   N   ♡ A J 8 4
              W   E   ◇ A 5 4
                   S   ♣ K 9 6 3
</pre>

West	North	East	South
	1♡	Pass	1♠
2♣	3♠	5♣	5♠
Pass	Pass	Double	All pass

West leads the ◇7: jack – ace – eight.
East switches to the ♣3, ruffed by South with the ♠6 – ♣2 – ♣10.
South plays the ♠J: ace – two – five.
West switches to the ♡9: king – ace – two.

What do you play next?

43. Teams: Dealer North : Nil vulnerable

Contract: 5♠ doubled   ♠ K 7 3 2
Lead: ◇7   ♡ K Q 10 7 6 5
                     ◇ K J
                     ♣ 10

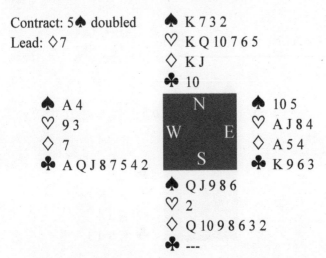

♠ A 4   ♠ 10 5
♡ 9 3   ♡ A J 8 4
◇ 7   ◇ A 5 4
♣ A Q J 8 7 5 4 2   ♣ K 9 6 3

                 ♠ Q J 9 8 6
                 ♡ 2
                 ◇ Q 10 9 8 6 3 2
                 ♣ ---

You know West began with eight clubs. Ignore the possibility that South began with a 6-2-5-0 pattern. In that case, West has no more trumps and you will not beat 5♠.

If South has a 5-2-6-0 pattern, you need to return a heart for partner to ruff. If South is 5-1-7-0, you can give West a diamond ruff. It is true that 5-2-6-0 is more common than 5-1-7-0, but there are two clues to the right answer. With two diamonds and one heart, why would West lead a doubleton and not the singleton?

A much stronger indication is in the early play. What did West play at trick 2? Yes, West played the ♣2, clearly a suit preference signal for the lowest other suit, diamonds. With a singleton heart, West could have the played the ♣A at trick 2.

In practice, East returned a heart and South escaped for one down, East-West +100, a loss of 5 Imps as the result in the same contract at the other table was two down, East-West +300.

A player who cannot defend accurately should strive to be declarer. (Alfred Sheinwold)

44. Teams: Dealer East : North-South vulnerable

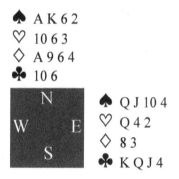

♠ A K 6 2
♡ 10 6 3
◇ A 9 6 4
♣ 10 6

♠ Q J 10 4
♡ Q 4 2
◇ 8 3
♣ K Q J 4

West	North	East	South
		Pass	1♣ (1)
Pass	1♠	Pass	2♠
Pass	3♠ (2)	Pass	3NT
Pass	Pass	Pass	

(1) 3+ clubs
(2) Inviting game

West leads the ♠5: two – ten – seven.
East switches to the ♣K: two – nine (high-encourage) – six.
What next?

44. Teams: Dealer East : North-South vulnerable

Contract: 3NT
Lead: ♠5

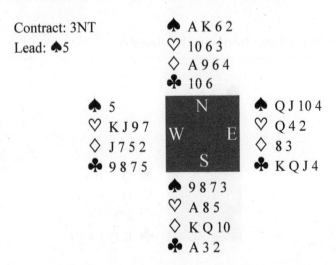

When West played the ♣9, encouraging, on East's ♣K switch, East placed West with ♣A-9-x and continued with a low club. South ducked and dummy's ♣10 won. South cashed the ♠A and West threw a heart. South played the ◇4 to the ◇K, followed by ◇Q and the ◇10, letting it run when West played low. South had two spades, a heart, four diamonds and two clubs, +600.

There was strong evidence that playing West for four clubs (continuing with ♣Q at trick 3) was better than hoping West had ♣A-9-x. If West had ♣A-9-x, South would have four clubs. If South's pattern was 3-3-3-4, South would rebid 1NT and not 2♠. If 4-3-2-4 or 4-2-3-4, South has a ruffing value in a red suit and would bid 4♠ over 3♠. This strongly suggests South is 4-3-3-3 with four spades. Further, would South duck at trick 1 if holding four rag clubs? Without the ♣A, South might well have ♡A-K-J, ◇K-Q-10 or similar and would win trick 1 and finesse the ♡J at trick 2 to play for two spades, three hearts and four diamonds.

My partner does not suffer commonsense gladly.

45. Teams: South dealer : East-West vulnerable

♠ K 10 4
♡ 10 9 6 5 2
♢ 8 7
♣ J 6 3

♠ Q 9 6 3
♡ Q 7 4
♢ J 10 5
♣ K 10 4

West	North	East	South
			1♣
1♢	Pass	Pass	2♠
Pass	4♠	All pass	

West leads the ♡K.
West continues with the ♡A, ruffed by declarer.
South plays the ♠2: jack – king – three.
South continues with dummy's ♣3: four – queen – nine.
South follows up with the ♣A: eight – six – ten, the ♢A, ♢K
(West playing ♢6 – ♢2) and the ♣2: ♢4 from West – ♣J – ♣K.

What should East do now?

45. Teams: South dealer : East-West vulnerable

Contract: 4♠
Lead: ♡K

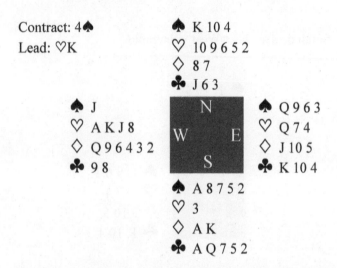

♠ K 10 4
♡ 10 9 6 5 2
♢ 8 7
♣ J 6 3

♠ J
♡ A K J 8
♢ Q 9 6 4 3 2
♣ 9 8

♠ Q 9 6 3
♡ Q 7 4
♢ J 10 5
♣ K 10 4

♠ A 8 7 5 2
♡ 3
♢ A K
♣ A Q 7 5 2

Most prefer to open 1♠ with 5-5 in the black suits, but each to his own. After ♡K, ♡A, ruffed, ♠2 to the jack and king, ♣3 to the ♣Q, ♣A, ♢A, ♢K, South plays the ♣2: ♢4 – ♣J – ♣K.

In positions like this in the trump suit, it often pays you to play your high trump, the ♠Q. It does not cost a trick since the ♠9 becomes high anyway. If you play the ♠Q, South can win and play a club, discarding a heart from dummy. East ruffs and now plays the ♡Q. South ruffs and is left with a club and a trump. East has ♠9, ♢J. If South plays a trump to dummy's ♠10, West wins the last trick with a heart. If South plays a club and discards from dummy, East ruffs. If South plays the club and ruffs it, East's ♠9 is the fourth trick for the defence, too.

Incompitance. Who needs it! We got to do something about the ever-increasing incompitance in the bridge world, especially among it's writers. If we don't stop it now, its hardly never going to quit by isself. (Richard Pavlicek)

46. Teams: Dealer North : Both vulnerable

♠ K 10 3 2
♡ K Q 4 3 2
◇ Q
♣ 9 7 4

♠ 7 6 5
♡ A 9 6
◇ A K 9 5
♣ 8 5 2

West	North	East	South
	Pass	1◇	1NT
2◇	Double (1)	Pass	2NT
Pass	3♡ (2)	Pass	3NT
Pass	Pass	Pass	

(1) For takeout
(2) Shows five hearts

West leads the ◇6: queen – king – two.
East switches to the ♣8: jack – queen – four.
West shifts to the ♠9: two – seven – ace.
South plays the ♡5: jack – king . . .

Plan the defence for East.

46. Teams: Dealer North : Both vulnerable

Contract: 3NT
Lead: ◇6

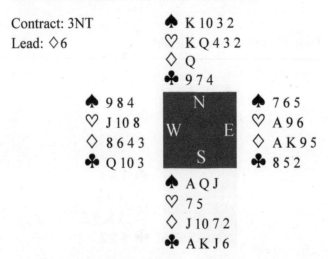

♠ K 10 3 2
♡ K Q 4 3 2
◇ Q
♣ 9 7 4

♠ 9 8 4
♡ J 10 8
◇ 8 6 4 3
♣ Q 10 3

♠ 7 6 5
♡ A 9 6
◇ A K 9 5
♣ 8 5 2

♠ A Q J
♡ 7 5
◇ J 10 7 2
♣ A K J 6

East's 1◇ opening and West's 2◇ over 1NT were bold (aka silly)
and are not recommended. 2◇ doubled would have cost 800.

Many pairs lead second-highest from three or four rag cards,
hence West's ◇6 lead. From South's 2NT and 3NT, East can
deduce that South began with ◇J-x-x-x and probably ◇J-10-x-x.
Continuing diamonds would help only South and so East switched
to a club at trick 2, the ♣8 to show no interest in clubs. After ♣Q,
West could have tried the ♡J, but that would have been foolish if
South had ♡A-x and East ♠A-Q. Hence West shifted to the ♠9.

Needing at least one trick from the hearts, South played the ♡5:
jack – king . . . If East ducks this, South can play a spade to the
♠Q and the ◇J. With the clubs 3-3, this would give South nine
tricks. East should take the ♡K with the ♡A and return the ♡6.
West's ♡J, either from J-10 doubleton or from J-10-8, was a most
helpful card for East. After the heart return, the defence will come
to five tricks before declarer can make nine.

*The Thinnest Bridge Book: Why Partner Should Feel Good About
His Defence.*

47. Teams: Dealer West : Nil vulnerable

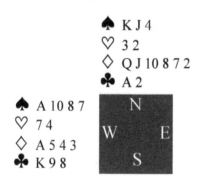

♠ K J 4
♡ 3 2
◇ Q J 10 8 7 2
♣ A 2

♠ A 10 8 7
♡ 7 4
◇ A 5 4 3
♣ K 9 8

West	North	East	South
Pass	1◇	2♣	2♡
3♣	Pass	Pass	3♡
Pass	Pass	Pass	

West leads the ♣8: ace – seven (low = encouraging) – ten.
The ♡2 is played from dummy: ten – king – four.
South continues with the ♡Q: seven – three – ace.
East plays the ◇K: six – five – two.
East switches the ♠5: three – ace – four.

What should West do now?

47. Teams: Dealer West : Nil vulnerable

Contract: 3♡
Lead: ♣8

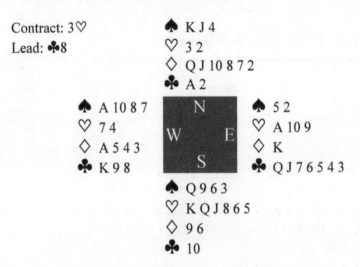

```
                    ♠ K J 4
                    ♡ 3 2
                    ◇ Q J 10 8 7 2
                    ♣ A 2
    ♠ A 10 8 7                      ♠ 5 2
    ♡ 7 4              N            ♡ A 10 9
    ◇ A 5 4 3      W       E        ◇ K
    ♣ K 9 8            S            ♣ Q J 7 6 5 4 3
                    ♠ Q 9 6 3
                    ♡ K Q J 8 6 5
                    ◇ 9 6
                    ♣ 10
```

After ♣8, won by ♣A, ♡2 to the king and the ♡Q to the ace, East switched to the ◇K, winning, and the ♠5 to West's ace.

West should deduce the following: (1) East's ◇K is a singleton, else East could continue diamonds. (2) East began with three trumps. With ♡A-9 doubleton and interested in a diamond ruff, East would take the ♡A at trick 2 and switch to the ◇K then. (3) East did not try to reach the West hand with a club. East must know that South is out of clubs and a club return would be futile.

West can thus piece together the East hand: 7 clubs because no club return + three hearts as above + the ◇K singleton = 11 cards and hence only two spades.

After ♠A, West should cash the ◇A. East discards the ♠2 and West gives East a spade ruff for one down. If West plays a low diamond at trick 6, East can ruff, but that is only four tricks for the defence. The defence needs to take the ◇A and score a ruff, too.

Bridge columnist: The Goof that Relays the Olden Gag.

48. Teams: Dealer East : North-South vulnerable

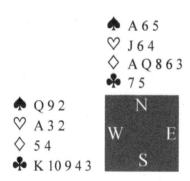

♠ A 6 5
♥ J 6 4
♦ A Q 8 6 3
♣ 7 5

♠ Q 9 2
♥ A 3 2
♦ 5 4
♣ K 10 9 4 3

West	North	East	South
		Pass	1♠
Pass	2♦	Pass	2♠
Pass	4♠	All pass	

West leads the ♣10: five – ace – two.
East returns the ♥10: seven – ace – four.

How would you continue as West?

48. Teams: Dealer East : North-South vulnerable

Contract: 4♠
Lead: ♣10

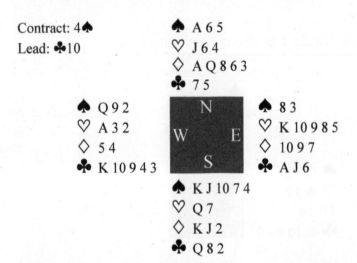

```
                    ♠ A 6 5
                    ♡ J 6 4
                    ◇ A Q 8 6 3
                    ♣ 7 5
    ♠ Q 9 2                         ♠ 8 3
    ♡ A 3 2          N              ♡ K 10 9 8 5
    ◇ 5 4        W       E          ◇ 10 9 7
    ♣ K 10 9 4 3     S              ♣ A J 6
                    ♠ K J 10 7 4
                    ♡ Q 7
                    ◇ K J 2
                    ♣ Q 8 2
```

The deal arose in the semi-finals of the 2000 World Mixed Teams.
One table stopped in 3♠. West led ◇5. South won, crossed to the
♠A and finessed ♠J. West won, cashed ♡A and ♣K and played
the ♣5. East's ♣A and ♡K meant one down. Had West not taken
the ♣K first, East might have tried to give West a diamond ruff.

The other three tables were in 4♠ after it began 1♠ : 2◇. One
West led the ♣10 to the ♣A, won the ♡10 with the ♡A, cashed
the ♣K and then returned a heart to the ♡K, East-West +100.

One West led ♣10 to ♣A. East returned ♣6. Thinking East was
out of clubs, West returned a club, ruffed in dummy. South played
◇K, ♠J winning, ♠A, ◇J, ♠K, diamonds, North-South +620.

The last West led ♣4 to the ♣A. East shifted to ♡10. West won
and instead of cashing the ♣K, returned a heart. East won and,
thinking West had no more hearts, played a third heart. South also
played West for the ♠Q and made ten tricks, North-South +620.

*When I mention suit-preference to my partner, he takes it as a
clothing hint.*

49. Teams: Dealer East : Both vulnerable

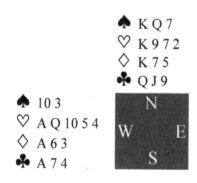

♠	K Q 7
♡	K 9 7 2
♢	K 7 5
♣	Q J 9

♠	10 3
♡	A Q 10 5 4
♢	A 6 3
♣	A 7 4

West	North	East	South
		Pass	1♠
2♡	4♠	All pass	

1. ♠3: king – five – two
2. ♠7: nine – jack – ten
3. ♡3: ace – two – eight (1)
4. ♣A: nine – eight – two
5. ♣7: jack – six – king
6. ♢8 from South . . .
(1) You play reverse count, if that is relevant.

What would you play as West?

49. Teams: Dealer East : Both vulnerable

Contract: 4 ♠   ♠ K Q 7
Lead: ♠3   ♡ K 9 7 2
                                ◇ K 7 5
                                ♣ Q J 9

```
        ♠ 10 3                  N                  ♠ 9 5
        ♡ A Q 10 5 4                              ♡ J 8 6
                           W         E
        ◇ A 6 3                                   ◇ J 10 9 4 2
        ♣ A 7 4                  S                 ♣ 8 6 3
```

                                ♠ A J 8 6 4 2
                                ♡ 3
                                ◇ Q 8
                                ♣ K 10 5 2

By trick 5, West has won two tricks. Is there any hope to beat 4♠?

East played ♠5 then ♠9, showing two spades, and so South has
six spades. South has two club tricks and the ♡K in dummy. If
West plays low on the diamond, dummy's ◇K will win and as
declarer has six spades, declarer has ten tricks no matter what. As
South opened, it is also very likely that South has the ◇Q.

Can it cost to duck? Sure. Dummy's ◇K wins and the ♡K allows
South to discard the ◇Q. Since ducking cannot gain, you should
grab the ◇A and hold South to ten tricks. At the table, West
ducked and declarer made eleven tricks, +650.

At the other table, after ♠3 to the ♠K, ♠7 to ♠J and ♡3 taken
by the ♡A, West switched to a low diamond. South won and
made eleven tricks, too, no swing. The margin in the match was
one Imp. Had West taken the ◇A at the other table, it would have
been a tie and more boards to be played.

The margin between success and drama is fractional. (Jacky Ickx)

50. Teams: Dealer South : North-South vulnerable

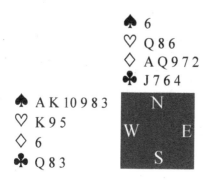

```
                        ♠ 6
                        ♡ Q 8 6
                        ♢ A Q 9 7 2
                        ♣ J 7 6 4
    ♠ A K 10 9 8 3           N
    ♡ K 9 5
    ♢ 6              W              E
    ♣ Q 8 3
                            S
```

West	North	East	South
			2♣ (1)
2♠	Double (2)	Pass	2NT
Pass	3NT	All pass	

(1) Precision System, 5+ clubs, 11-15 points
(2) For takeout

South's 2♣ opening showed either 6+ clubs with no second suit or 5+ clubs and a 4-card suit. What would you lead as West?

Suppose you have chosen the ♠A and it goes six, five, four. What would you play next?

50. Teams: Dealer South : North-South vulnerable

Contract: 3NT
Lead: ♠10? / ♠A?

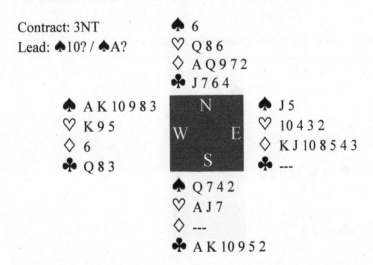

```
                        ♠ 6
                        ♡ Q 8 6
                        ◇ A Q 9 7 2
                        ♣ J 7 6 4
     ♠ A K 10 9 8 3          N          ♠ J 5
     ♡ K 9 5                            ♡ 10 4 3 2
     ◇ 6                  W       E      ◇ K J 10 8 5 4 3
     ♣ Q 8 3                 S          ♣ ---
                        ♠ Q 7 4 2
                        ♡ A J 7
                        ◇ ---
                        ♣ A K 10 9 5 2
```

The deal arose in the qualifying stage of a National Seniors' Team Selection. South made 3NT when West did not find the best series of plays. If West starts with the ♠10, clearly from an interior sequence, East should contribute the ♠J to clarify the position for partner. That would lead easily to two down.

The actual lead was the ♠A. Had West continued with a top spade at trick 2 or had East played the ♠J under the ♠A (hard to do), that would also produce two down. West elected to try to find East's entry at trick two and switched to the ♡5: six – ten – jack. South played the ♣A, followed by a low club. West won and, hoping that East had started with ♡A-10-x-x or similar, continued with the ♡K at trick 4. That meant +600 to North-South and +9 Imps against the datum of North-South 230. Had West taken 3NT two down for +200, it would have been +10 Imps for East-West.

Successful defence produces a significantly bigger high than skilful declarer play.

A Bonus Puzzle:

Teams: Dealer North : Nil vulnerable

```
              ♠ 9 8 5
              ♡ A K 10 3
              ◇ K Q 7
              ♣ 10 9 7
         ┌─────────────┐
         │      N      │
         │  W       E  │
         │      S      │
         └─────────────┘
              ♠ A K 7 4 2
              ♡ 6
              ◇ A 10 6
              ♣ A K Q 5
```

West	North	East	South
	1♣ (1)	Pass	1♠
Pass	1NT	Pass	3♣
Pass	3♠	Pass	4NT
Pass	5◇ (2)	Pass	5♡ (3)
Pass	5♠ (4)	Pass	6♠
Pass	Pass	Pass	

(1) Playing 5-card majors and a strong 1NT
(2) One key card for spades
(3) 'Do you have the queen of trumps?'
(4) 'No.'

1. West leads ♡Q: ace – two – six
2. Declarer plays the ♠5: three – ace – jack.

How would you continue as South?

Teams: Dealer North : Nil vulnerable

Contract: 6♠
Lead: ♡Q

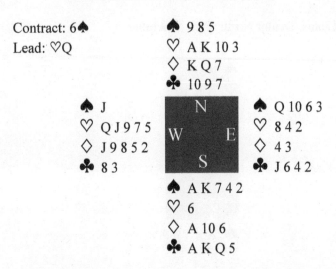

The slam depends essentially on a 3-2 break in spades. However, because of your good intermediate trumps (the ♠9, ♠8 and ♠7), you can cater for some 4-1 splits. While the 3-2 break is very likely (around 68%), the chance of a 4-1 break is about 28%, a figure that is high enough for you to take precautions if possible.

When West drops an honour card under your ace at trick 2, simply continue with a low spade to the ♠9. If trumps do split 3-2, you can win any return and play the ♠K to mop up the missing trump. When West shows out and East captures dummy's ♠9, you win, say, a club and play a low diamond to dummy and the ♠8, winning when East plays low. Return to hand with a low heart, ruffed, cash the ♠K and claim, your fourth club going on the ♡K.

Of course, if you did play ♠A and ♠K, you will be one down and deserve to be so.

If you take a safety play, it wasn't necessary. If you fail to take a safety play, it was necessary.

You will not find the bonus puzzle in

50 Great Puzzles on Declarer Play

by Ron Klinger

Weidenfeld & Nicolson
in association with
PETER CRAWLEY

but you will find fifty other entertaining and instructive puzzles on declarer play there (and a bonus puzzle on defence, too).